MUD AND KH

# MUD AND KHAKI

*The Memories of an Incomplete Soldier*

by

## H. S. CLAPHAM
(The Honourable Artillery Company)

The thanks of the Author are due to Major Charles Reid, D.S.O. and Mr. R. P. FLACK for permission to use the photographs reproduced in this book.

The Château Stables, Hooge, July, 1915

[Frontispiece

# LIST OF PLATES

The Château Stables, Hooge, July, 1915 . . *Frontispiece*

Facing
page

"K2"—a so-called trench in front of Kemmel, February, 1915 . . . . . . 20

A corner in the "P" trenches opposite the "Mound", St. Eloi, April, 1915 . . . . . 36

Street scenes in Ypres after the Second Bombardment, July, 1915 . . . . . . . 46

In Maple Copse, Hooge, June, 1915 . . . 60

"Y" Wood, Hooge, during the attack on June 16th, 1915 . . . . . . . . 72
*(From a film found on the body of a soldier killed on that day.)*

Communication Trench, Sanctuary Wood, June, 1915 88

The Great Crater at Hooge . . . . . 96

The Menin Road, September, 1915 . . . . 108

Front-line trench, Sanctuary Wood, near Hooge, July, 1915 . . . . . . . 122

"The Wall", near Hooge, taken from front line in Sanctuary Wood, July 2nd, 1915 . . . 136

The Crater Trench, Hooge, September, 1915 . . 160

Rest Field at Booseboom, near Dickebusche, September, 1915 . . . . . . . 174

Rest Field at Ouderdom, August 20th, 1915 . . 174

The Apex Trench, Sanctuary Wood, Hooge, September, 1915 . . . . . . . 190

Signallers' dugout, Sanctuary Wood, Hooge, September, 1915 . . . . . . . 202

Dugouts in Maple Copse, Hooge, October, 1915 . 214

# MUD AND KHAKI

13th January, 1915.

We marched over the shoulder of Kemmel Hill in full view of the Hun lines and in broad daylight. Later we found that this was a breach of the local rules, but being a new draft and nobody's children we didn't know and we didn't care.

It had rained all day, and the march from the "Vinery" at Bailleul, where we had spent the previous night, had been on the slippery *pavé* all the way. In a soggy farmsteading, where we had halted for a meal, I had been physically sick with fatigue; and this was really hardly to be wondered at, for the added weight of a mackintosh cape, a goatskin coat, pack, webbing, and ammunition, weighed to the ground men who, until the eve of their departure for France a fortnight before, had carried nothing more than rifles and rolled coats.

We were very green. Rifles and ammunition had been served out to us at Southampton, but no man knew his own weapon or had ever used it. We had spent a fortnight on the road, herded in cattle trucks, "*Hommes* 40, *Chevaux* 8", lying in six inches of mud at Sanvic Rest Camp, unloading bags of oats at Rouen quay, and all the time half-starved, owing partly, it is true, to the inefficiency of our amateur cooks, who understood more of carburetters or contangos than New Zealand mutton.

Now we felt we were entering the promised land, and the view towards the east, flat and uninteresting as it looked in the grey mist of rain, was apparently peaceful enough.

At the foot of the hill we wound on to the village green of Kemmel. In the centre stood a dilapidated bandstand, and on the rough triangle of turf around it were stacks of barbed wire, knife rests—giant reproductions of those which flank the joint in the commercial room—bundles of brushwood or fascines, spades, and all sorts of engineers' stores. The houses around were more or less in ruins and the village was evidently abandoned.

Here we halted. No one seemed to expect us. Not a soul was to be seen, and it was some time before we found an officer who could give instructions as to where we were to be stowed away. At last, however, we moved again, and, turning to the left, took possession of some ruins in the outskirts of the village, where we made ourselves as comfortable as circumstances would allow.

With five others I became the tenant of a small room, almost whole, about eight feet square. Two small shell-holes in the walls were covered up with sacking. A waterproof sheet hung across the empty window-frame, and a tiled floor made a dry, if stony bed. Operations commenced with the usual fatigue of obligation—latrine digging—but in a very short time we were free to look after ourselves.

The ruins were full of debris, and with old chair-legs, gate-posts, and other relics, we soon managed to get a fire going on the hearth. There was nothing much in our own garden, but adjoining was a strip of old allotment ground, and a foraging expedition quickly produced potatoes, onions, and mixed green stuff. The resulting stew of bully beef and vegetables was quite good.

Just up the road we discovered two cottages still occupied by ancient smoke-dried crones, who were quite prepared to sell us hot black coffee, and those round flat loaves of Flemish bread which are quite eatable when fresh, but quickly harden into the consistency of granite. I was warm enough that night and slept as soundly as any-one could wish.

*17th January*, 1915.

At last we have got into the midst of it. The morning after we arrived in Kemmel we spent on fatigue mud-slinging, i.e., cleaning the roads. Being nobody's children still, we had to fend for ourselves in every way; but it was rather fun. About two o'clock I was startled by a crash and saw a cloud of smoke on the hill-top. The Huns were shelling. Within the next quarter of an hour about seven big Jack Johnsons exploded on the hill about half-a-mile away. They told us that this happened every day at two, with the precision of clockwork. One can hear the shells passing over with a roar, but no one takes much notice, and they do no apparent harm, except to the trees.

In the evening about two hundred men went off on a carrying fatigue to the Redoubt, but none of our party was taken, so having foraged again, we had another stew, and were getting nicely warm around the fire, when about seven p.m. a banging at the door preceded a call for "ten men wanted for fatigue". Four of us were ordered to parade at once with rifles and ten

rounds each. We felt our way out in the darkness and found an officer waiting for us down
the road.

We were ordered to load, and I got into
trouble at once. My rifle had obviously never
been loaded in its little life and I could not force
the clip of cartridges into the magazine. Of
course, I got cursed roundly, but after an unsuccess-
ful attempt by the officer to remedy the trouble,
I was sent back to borrow a fresh rifle. When
I rejoined them, our squad was marched off in
the darkness past buildings which one could sense
rather than see, and up a sort of drive to the door
the local Château. We were challenged at the
entrance and then taken into a large hall, in the
centre of which stood a red velvet settee, apparently the sleeping-place of the corporal of the
guard. In one corner of the hall lay the iron
standard of a big pump, some lengths of hosepipe and other parts.

A N.C.O. received us. " You are to take the
pump up to the trenches. We have a guide for
you. Report when you return." Four of us
took up the standard by the handles fixed at the
side. It was about three feet long and very heavy.
I got a roll of hosepipe which I managed to hitch
over one shoulder.

Off we went again into the dark, stumbling

over the broken *pavé* of the village street and out into the open country. Nowhere was there a sign of life other than the sudden gleam of a star-shell in the distance. A few minutes later there was a curious hissing in the air and something hit the road. A spent bullet. One realized that for the first time one was in the fire zone, and thereupon came a slightly uncomfortable feeling in the pit of one's stomach. The further we went the more bullets we met; but the hiss became a wail, and every now and then a sound, like the mewing of a cat, which is made by a ricochet.

Occasionally a star-shell rose like a rocket in front and burst into a flare of light, showing up the road as it sank slowly to the ground. The track of a light railway ran by the side of the road, but the rails were bent and twisted into fantastic shapes, and here and there the road itself disappeared into a huge crater. We stumbled over a dead horse, half on and half off the track. It was all rather weird; the lights, the single rifle-shots, and the blackness of desolation all around.

At length, for we could only travel slowly, we reached a building of some sort. Half the front had gone and the roof hung down over a gap at one end. Our guide murmured something to the glowing end of a cigarette which appeared in the darkness and received a reply: "No talking and go quickly past the corner. It is marked by a sniper and a man was killed there only an hour ago." This is the debateable land and no man passes there by day. The dead lie unburied in the fields on either side, but at night the road becomes alive with hurrying shadows, reliefs, fatigues, and the silent bearers of the dead and wounded.

We reached the top of a rise and a low voice came out of the darkness: "Who goes there?" "Fatigue." "Pass." By this time I had given up my hosepipe and was attached to a handle of the standard. If one bearer stumbled, my hand was nearly broken by the edge of the iron plate. As we were getting near the trenches, every time a star-shell flared we had to stop and fall on one knee until the light faded again.

A whisper came from the front: "Slowly here, there's a hole in front". The hole had been partly filled with brick ends and covered with loose timbers, but one board turned over under my foot and I went in up to the knee, whilst the standard came to the ground, amidst muttered curses from the others. For the next twenty yards there was no road and we scrambled along as best we could.

We seemed to be going down-hill, for every now and then we could see a spurt of fire, apparently below us, and all the time the rifles kept up a sort of irregular rattle. Suddenly there was a deeper, more metallic explosion. " Trench mortar," whispered the guide. The bullets seemed to be playing all around us. If one seemed to pass close by, we ducked involuntarily, but we were not conscious of any fear, or even of fatigue. Everything was so new and weird that we were too much interested.

" Lie down when a star-shell rises. We are close there now and the German lines are only fifty yards beyond." As the word came a star-shell rose and before the light flared out we were lying on our stomachs in several inches of mud and water. One could feel the clammy wet coming through to one's flesh. Again we were up and on. " Who's that?" came in a low tone from the roadside. " You are going too far; the entrance is here." We turned off the road to the left and scrambled between two mounds of clay into the trench.

Here and there bucket braziers were burning, and dark figures, muffled to the eyes and looking in the glow like souls in Hell, were gathered about them. Every now and then a figure standing on the fire-step and only half-visible, leaned over the parapet and fired, and every now and then a bullet from the other side buried itself with a thud in the sandbags. With aching arms we placed our burdens against the side of the trench, and the corporal disappeared into a lighted hole, beneath the parados, to report to the officer in charge. We talked to the men around. They told us they had had a quiet night so far, and gave us a drink of hot tea brewed on the brazier. " Take care when you leave. There's a Hun post twenty yards away."

The corporal returned and we filed out again, but just as we stepped on to the road, a star-shell burst and we had to throw ourselves on our faces. The Huns must have heard or seen something, for a regular fusilade broke out and star-shell followed star-shell in quick succession. The bullets seemed to whistle just over our heads and we lay for ten minutes, soaking up mud and water. Then the uproar died down and we got to our feet and hurried on. Four times at least in a hundred yards, we had to throw ourselves on the ground again, but by degrees we got past the crest of the ridge, and from that point a friendly hedge more or less screened us from view.

The trip took us three hours and we returned wet through with water and sweat and with no chance of a change, a wash, or a dry before the morning; but, to a beginner, it was quite an interesting evening.

The next morning I found that the lower part of my greatcoat, which reached to the ankles, was a solid board of mud, and as it was not dry enough to scrape, it had at least doubled in weight. As I had found the tails a great nuisance the previous night—for one trips on them when trying to get to one's feet—I cut off a foot length around the bottom. It is not so warm at night as it was, but much more comfortable in every other respect.

That morning we foraged round the village, although this was another breach of the local rules. There is rather a fine old church with a big clock. The Château is the property of an Austrian Count, and there is a nice-looking châlet which was occupied by his mother, or some other relative. In the garden of the latter we secured quite a variety of vegetables and fared sumptuously on the proceeds.

In the evening, a lot of us went up on fatigue to our own trenches. This time we picked up bundles of fascines and a heavy door. My own bundle was most insecurely bound and most difficult to carry, and I was given a change to the door half-way up. From my own point of

view the change was not a success, as there was
nothing on the door to hold on to and the
wretched thing was always falling, because the
fingers of some bearer refused to carry on any
longer. We went up the same road but turned
to the right at the trench line instead of to the
left. It was a quiet night, but by the time we
got back I was done to the world and sodden
with sweat.

Yesterday after dark the battalion came out
to rest, and we all marched to Locre, three miles
in the rear. As nobody's children, we were
shoved in anywhere. About thirty of us were
billeted in a curious erection, half-barn, half-oast
house. At each end was an open barn or stable,
and between them, a sort of tunnel or heating
chamber, about five feet high and with air shafts
to the roof. With seven others I lay in the tunnel
and, as it was snowing heavily and a gale was
blowing down from end to end, we awoke in the
morning covered with a thin coating of snow.

All Sunday morning I was shovelling snow
in the village street. It wasn't a bad little place,
and I managed to get a hot drink at a café and
later on share a bottle of red wine. I felt quite
fit; but snow-shovelling is a wet enough job for
anyone.

On the 18th our draft was paraded and split up between the different companies and platoons. Two of our little lot have joined the Signallers, but the other five of us are all together in one section. We did not actually join our company until we returned to Kemmel, two days later, and by that time I had had quite enough of my oast house. I never before struck any place so cold!

Marching to Kemmel we must have looked like a set of scarecrows. Every man had a bulging pack and was hung round with tins, bits of wood for firing, and all sorts of odds and ends. Some wore balaclava helmets, and one sportsman a sort of Cossack headgear of fur.

My own company was not in the trenches the first night, and I was detailed as one of the guard at the Château. It was a lonely job, but there was nothing much to do, and when off duty, I got a rest on the velvet settee in the hall. The next day I felt very sick and evidently had a chill on the liver, the result probably of the oast house. I looked so bad that they would not take me up with them to the trenches. I went on fatigue, carrying bags of coke and charcoal, but returned at once and was sick most of the night. Luckily, we had a dry billet with a wooden floor. Another of our new men was down with the same complaint, but he was much worse than I, and could do little else than lie and groan.

I was a trifle better in the morning, and in the evening was on fatigue again, this time carrying sandbags to the trenches of a Lancashire battalion. It was a rotten trip, chiefly across country. We had to pass down a lane known as Frenchmen's Lane. One ditch had been converted into a trench by the French, and the lane was a mound of slippery clay, which had been the parapet. The path was on the ridge of this mound, and one was constantly slipping, either towards the trench, which stank to Heaven, or towards the ditch on the other side. At intervals were unburied French bodies, which sometimes I could just see, looking up at me in the light of the flares.

Beyond the lane we passed round some farm buildings and through a gate—"Hell's Gate"— a rather nasty place for bullets, and then across several fields, which seemed to be a network of ditches, crossed sometimes by single planks, which one felt for but could not see. I did not feel

up to much when I got back, but I managed
to fill and light a bucket brazier. After half
an hour's swinging, I got it to burn, more
or less, so that when the troops returned from
the trenches there was a fire and a hot drink all
round.

I was all right again the next day, and at night
went up for my first turn of trench duty with
the company. We held a front-line trench which
had only recently been dug by the Engineers and
is supposed to be one of the best around here. It
is comparatively dry, and there are a fair number
of dugouts, little cubby-holes in the parados, into
which two or three men can just curl themselves.
Although we were about 80 yards from the Huns,
we could see nothing of them but a mound of
earth and sandbags. For some reason or other
they shove in a black sandbag here and there
amongst the others, so the mound looks as if it
were spotted with black boulders.

I was on guard for an hour three times during
the night, and in accordance with instructions
fired a round at nothing every ten minutes or so.
Apparently it is quite safe to keep your head over
the parapet at night, if you duck when a star-
shell flares to the ground. It is impossible to see
anything sufficiently clearly to aim straight. I
turned in in a dugout for a couple of hours. The

atmosphere was as thick as a London fog, but I believe I actually slept a bit.

The other men in the section are the nicest chaps I have met in this game, and we have really quite a good time.

The morning was fine, with a bright sun and a touch of frost. Always at dawn we stand to for half an hour, with rifles ready, in case of attack. But that is merely the usual routine. Then we can get breakfast—Flemish bread, jam, sardines, and a rasher of bacon fried on the section brazier. We seemed to be at the bottom of a shallow valley, with the Huns just above us in front, and our own support line, also above us, a hundred yards to the rear. Breakfast was evidently proceeding in the support line, for the smoke from half a dozen braziers curled up into the frosty air. Above, on the ridge, was the skeleton of a farmhouse, and on its left a clump of trees, beneath which lay three bodies in uniforms of red and blue.

The morning was very quiet. There was hardly a rifle shot and never a shell, until early in the afternoon they started to shell the ruins of the farmhouse and our support trench with what were stated to be six-inch howitzers. When we can hear the shell coming, we get down as low as we can in the trench. If it passes over, we can actually see it falling through the air. We look up for a second to see where it falls; but down we must go again at once for fear of flying fragments.

I was much interested at first, and our platoon sergeant noticed it. " I suppose you find this sort of thing interesting, but the more you see of it the less you'll like it." Just then the shells began to fall much nearer. One burst only twenty-five yards away and covered us with dirt and debris. The next seemed to fall right in the trench, but fifty yards further to the north. I could see timbers and all sorts of things flying through the air.

Just at our back was a series of drainage trenches, and five minutes later a little dark man without a cap scrambled over these and made a dash for our trench. Immediately after there appeared over a mound of earth a broad grinning face, surmounted by a mop of red hair, and by its side was an enormous kettle held high in the air. The owner of these advanced more slowly. He explained that the shell had arrived in his transverse just as he had made tea. As the latter had not suffered, he had escaped, carrying his tea with him, along the back of our trench, until he saw a chance of entering it and drinking in peace. They shared the kettle with us and kept us in roars of laughter for half an hour, after which they returned to their own people by the way they had come. Luckily, the shelling had ceased, but, anyway, red-head was a great man.

I was on guard just as it was getting too dark to see. I was watching through a loophole, when, in the dim light, I saw ten Huns running along the skyline. My wretched rifle misfired, and as no one else saw them they all jeered at me for seeing things that weren't there. We all prepared for a possible attack, but nothing happened.

A lot of misfires had been reported, and we were kept busy for some time, sorting over ammunition, in order that certain marks of American manufacture, which were supposed to be imperfect, might be returned to store for inspection.

We were relieved about 6 p.m. on the 24th
and marched back to Locre. Our billet was a
room with a stone floor in a corner *estaminet,*
just opposite the church. I was so done in when
we arrived, that I almost collapsed on the floor,
and I think I should have slept in my equipment
if a side door had not opened and a voice said:
" Cheer-o, boys. Just drink this with the South
Lancs." It was a sergeant of that regiment,
and "this" was a large jug of Flemish beer.
He was some Samaritan, and I never in my
life found a drink go down so well. After
that I succeeded in struggling out of my equipment and slept for eleven hours on the stone
floor.

My hands have got very sore with the wet and
their unaccustomed labours, but I suppose they
will get used to things in time. Half the
battalion is "standing by", which means ready to
march at fifteen minutes' notice and entails,
amongst other distresses, the necessity of sleeping in boots. In fact, we usually take them off;
but whoever is found out is "for it".

I was on billet guard all one day, and yesterday we were route-marched round the country and through a village called West-outre, where I saw the Canadian troops for the first time. To-day we had a pay parade, at which I drew the handsome sum of five francs.

Each platoon has its favoured *estaminet*. Ours is known as "Emma's", the name of the sturdy wench who, with her sister Albertine, appears to run the show. One can get *soupe-au-lait*, which is bread and milk, and a sort of jumble of fried eggs, which they call an omelette. There is also hot coffee and sour wine and Flemish beer, none of which I am at all keen on, and they will always cook anything we like to buy. The great thing about the place is that we can get near a stove which is usually red hot.

As all our men cannot get into the billet, some sleep in the church across the road. There they have to turn out at an unearthly hour of the morning in order to make room for a service. We usually wash, stripped to the waist, at the parish pump, where some washing troughs have been erected. The only chance of a bath is to go to a cottage and pay for a bucket of hot water and the use of a tub in the kitchen. It is a very public ceremonial, but it would require much more than the spectacle of soldiers bathing to upset the stolidity of these Flemish peasants. So far I am free from lice, but that plague is almost universal. One cannot walk down the village street without seeing two or more mothers busily occupied with the heads of their off-spring. It is rather like the monkey-house at the Zoo.

4th February, 1915.

We returned to the line on the 28th, but our first night was in reserve in Kemmel village. Our billet there, this time, was the chapel of St. Germanus's Schools, which are still in a fair condition. Although it was a very cold and draughty spot, the wooden floor was comfortable. I lay alongside X—who came out with me—and, at his suggestion, we exchanged home addresses, with the arrangement that if one of us should retire hurt, the other would write to his people.

Kemmel is reviving. There are at least three cottages where coffee can be found, and the local post office has re-opened, not, of course, in its original capacity, but for the sale of what are called "Kemmel Fish". If one feels like it, one can stroll down to the post and sit down to a dinner-plate of custard, made in a mould, in the shape of a large fish. It really isn't half-bad, but as strolling is officially banned, the trip must be made with circumspection, or an errand must be improvised to the M.O. or the Quartermaster's Stores.

About midday on the 29th there were several

nasty explosions in the village. The Huns had put one or two shells into the cross-roads near our last billet. Two houses occupied by men of a north-country battalion were destroyed, and as the men were indoors at the time, we heard they lost nine killed and thirteen wounded. Although we were only a quarter of a mile away, it was evening before we could learn full details, as news only filters in through orderlies and fatigue men. I had a stroll up the road to the north, until I was told I was in full view of German territory and turned back by a picket. I had a look round the church, too. There are a number of tombstones to the memory of certain Jans and Hans, who are described as of "Wyper", from which it would appear that Tommy is, after all, justified in his speech.

We went into the front-line that night, but to a different trench, the next one to the south. The march up was across country, and though there were fewer bullets flying, it was far more exhausting. This country seems to have been devoted to turnips or beet, and when the under surface is frozen hard, with a covering of slimy clay and hard turnips, which cannot be seen in the dark, one trips and stumbles at every step. The French lost heavily here in the autumn, and one is always liable to step on or into something that was once a soldier.

A corner in the "P" Trenches opposite the "Mound", St. Eloi,
April, 1915

[To face page 36

Remember, too, that in addition to full equipment, a rifle and the regulation number of rounds, a goatskin coat and an army greatcoat, we carry up packs, full of the contents of our home parcels, and each man has slung over his shoulder one or more usually two sacks of rations, coke or charcoal, intended for the comfort of his own section or of the officers' mess.

Except on moonlight nights, as often as not, we can hardly see the next man ahead. We step into ditches with a jerk that brings us to our knees, and we have to climb out somehow on the other side. We barge through broken hedges, and if a thorn detains, we lose touch at once. The only warning is a whisper passed down the line: "Step down, ditch in front"; "Step up, tree across the path"; or "Stream in front, single plank". That is where a trench-stick with a club point is useful. Out here I have learnt the full meaning of the expression "Muck sweat". It is my usual condition.

Just at the back of the trenches we passed through a farmyard. Here we could see quite clearly in the light of the flares. We rounded a haystack, about which lay the bodies of three cows and some pigs, left behind, I suppose, in the flight of their owners, and dead from starvation or chance bullets.

The new trench ("F.2") was a rotten one, and as soon as we arrived we were warned to keep our heads down, as the parapet was low and weak in many places, and one or two spots were specially marked by snipers. As usual, we were in the low ground, and in many places the trench was a foot deep in water. Out of it opened little traverses which were not quite so wet, and most of them had a little shelter at each end, with a sort of thatch of wattle and straw.

They say this trench was originally a German one and was then held by the French, but whoever were the original owners, they were nasty people. When I arrived I was absolutely exhausted, and not being on guard, I crawled into one of the shelters. A few minutes' rest was what I wanted, but the place stank like a charnel-house, and I was very nearly sick before I could gather enough strength to crawl out again. Apparently the Huns used the bodies of the dead to form the nucleus of the parapet, and the resulting stench is horrible. In some places can be seen a foot or a hand sticking out of the trench wall, and one's hands stink from the mud which clings to them. My own are quite done in now. They get caked with this mud, and I can't wash, so the finger-tips fester and burst. It is painful to put my hands in my pocket.

We worked hard all night. A dozen yards at the back of the trench was a ruined cottage with unlimited supplies of brick-ends, and, unless I was actually doing my turn on guard, I filled sandbags with broken bricks and carried them into the trench to reinforce and raise the parapet. Brick-ends are not very suitable material, but for the moment, at any rate, the position was improved, and, in any case, the ground was too hard for digging.

The dawn came with a thick white mist, but in a short time a brilliant sun burst through. It rendered everything more slimy than ever, but things were quiet, and in the crisp air one felt it good to be alive.

My own little lot were having a very jolly meal of tea, tinned salmon, jam and biscuits, sitting round a brazier. X had his back to the parapet. We are always on the look-out for new sights, and some miles to the north, right up the trench, I saw a large captive balloon. We were all watching it, discussing if it were British or Hun, when there was a sudden crack, and X—who had risen to his feet—kicked the brazier over and fell back on to another man, who caught him in his arms. For a second one hardly realized what had happened, but the salmon on my biscuit was speckled red and white, and as we laid X down, we saw a furrow across the back of his head, from which the brains protruded. I don't think he could have felt anything at all, but he made inarticulate noises for three parts of an hour before he died. Poor K—who caught him as he fell, is very young and could do nothing but lean against the parapet and say " Oh, God!" It was the first time I had seen death in war-time, and it was upsetting even to me.

We did what we could, but that was nothing, and a medical orderly, who crawled over from another trench, could do no more. We laid the body on the low part of the parados, for nothing could be done until night. Neither the M.O. nor the stretcher-bearers could come up from Kemmel in daylight. After dark we carried him to the cottage at the back of the trench. There, in the tiny garden in which already five graves had been dug, we dug another in haste, amid flying bullets and in the light of the star-shells. We laid him there, whilst a private, who was also in Orders, recited the Burial Service. It was horribly impressive. Someone made a cross of sticks and placed it at the head of the grave.

We returned to Kemmel that night. I felt more dead than alive myself, but slept for hours like a log, and in the morning was on fatigue, cleaning out ruined houses for use as billets. It was not heavy work, luckily, for after dark we again relieved another company in the same trench as before. It was a beautiful moonlight night, and we worked like devils at sandbag-filling until dawn. Once we had to break it off in a hurry and take our places at the parapet. Very heavy firing broke out a bit to the north and rolled right down the line, until it reached us. We thought it might be an attack, but it proved to be merely one of the usual panics, which the Army calls "s—— fights", and all was quiet again in twenty minutes or so.

All day we spent trying to drain the trench, digging sump holes, with coverings of old doors or planks, but the water seemed to gather again as quickly as we got rid of it. We were not relieved until 7.30 p.m., and then had the two miles of muddy fields and another three or four of slippery *pavé*, off which we stumbled in the dark, into a foot or more of mud and slush. We got a drink of hot tea and rum from the cookers, which came down to Kemmel Village, on the way through, but it was ten before we reached Locre, and we were pretty well "all out" in the end. I suppose that when I get more used to it I shall stand it better, but the constant strain, the bent-double attitude of the day-time and the carrying fatigues of the night, are at present almost too much for me. I succeed in carrying on so long as I must, but on the march back, my tongue gets out of control, and I am told that then my language is the limit. At any rate, I have the utmost sympathy with "our armies in Flanders" two hundred years ago.

As soon as I got in I fell asleep in my equipment and boots on the stone floor of the billet, but fifteen hours later I was myself again, having eaten, shaved, bathed in a bucket of hot water, and had my hair clipped to the skull. It is true the short hairs stand on end, and the cap, resting on them, irritates the head, but it has the advantage of cleanliness at least. Before tubbing I caught a glimpse of myself in the cottage mirror. I had a five days' growth of beard, and as I had not washed during a couple of days of muck and sweat, the picture was an appalling one.

A new draft has arrived for the battalion, and includes a number of old friends. It is only six weeks or so since we left them in town, but they tell us that most of us have aged many years in that period. I am supposed to be the only one who has not altered much.

We leave to-night for the trenches again, and most of us are far from comfortable. An epidemic of mild diarrhœa has broken out, and nothing seems to stop it. It would be bad enough at home.

Out here, several times in a night, one has to step over sleeping men in the dark, and wander in the cold, down a lane and into a snow-covered field, where the local lavatory is represented by a series of open trenches. I went to the M.O., but all he could do was to give me a No. 9 pill —the universal specific of the Army. I trust I shall be better before reaching the front-line, as the accommodation there is far worse, and one is always rather liable to stop a bullet.

We had a rather good battalion concert in the local school the other evening. Quite a number of our men are almost professionals, and usually there is at least one topical song, written for the occasion. The Brigadier was present and appeared to appreciate. For two days we were "standing by", as usual, but one can always get a game of bridge or nap, and, in spite of discomforts, this rest has been fairly cheerful. So far as feeding goes, we do better than at any time since I joined up. A tin of Maconochie rations curried is far better than that somewhat sickly article in its native state, and with a little jam as a substitute for chutney, it is quite good eating. Pork chops can be bought; eggs are cheap, and soup is generally on tap in our particular *estaminet*.

The thing I hanker for is a pint of good English beer. The local drinks are rotten. Our water is mixed with chloride of lime, and the only "real thing" is the Army rum. It warms one when soaked to the skin. It revives one at one's worst, and without it I doubt if I could bear up at all on the long march "home". In a local shop I found a sort of tin bottle, which I can attach to my belt. In this is carried a good part of the section's rum, which is served out before we leave for the trenches. As I carry it, and several of the men don't drink it, I can generally reserve a little for the last march, which I have almost come to dread. Unfortunately, the bottle leaks slightly, but no one will believe that.

*13th February,* 1915.

We had a rather unpleasant four days "in". We marched down through Kemmel, but turned in through the Château grounds, and after branching off into the fields, found ourselves billeted for a couple of days, in reserve, in a hayloft overlooking an evil-smelling farmyard. The farm stands on a low ridge, in full view of the German lines. and we were not allowed outside in the daytime, lest movement should be observed and shelling follow. The farmer and his family were more friendly than usual, but foully dirty, and though we could get hot coffee, we hesitated to drink it. One of the family was a half-witted child.

They tell a story of one farm near here, where the barn became untenable, and on investigation the straw on the floor disclosed several unburied bodies of French soldiers, which had been left behind by their comrades. This hayloft might be equally bad. My own trouble is worse, and if one wanders out at night there are always many bullets about. Half-spent bullets are constantly burying themselves in our wooden walls, and some come right through. The only relief one could get was a game of cards and an evening fatigue for rations or water.

The "Old Man" came round the first evening, to see how we were getting on. He is a jolly good sort and quite capable of keeping up our end, as well as his own, with the powers-that-be.

On the evening of the 7th we relieved a battalion of the Middlesex in the "K" trenches. We started at 5.30 p.m., but had to call at Kemmel for rations and trench stores. I carried a spade as an extra to the usual sack of rations. After leaving Kemmel, our way was mostly across country. It was pitch dark and blew a gale with pelting rain. It was almost impossible to see the man in front, and I was so over-weighted that I could not keep my feet. Someone at home had sent me a most comfortable pair of gum boots, and these I was wearing instead of boots; but they would not grip, and after falling into a ditch I came to my knees in a stream of water. One man fell out in front with a bullet through his knee, and, as I passed, the stretcher-bearers were preparing to carry him to the dressing-station.

We had a long halt in the rain, while a detachment was taken off to man a redoubt, but we moved off at last through fields pitted with water-filled shell-holes. The star-shells seemed to be going up on three sides of us, but by their light

Street scenes in Ypres after the Second Bombardment, July, 1915

[To face page 46

it was much easier to travel. At last we reached a gap in a thick hedge. The man in front of me disappeared, and almost at once I heard a splash and a grunt as he took a header into a shell-crater on the far side. I got into the ditch and managed to pull myself and my burdens through the hedge. I never saw the crater, but no one was in sight. There was a faint light ahead, so I led on and found it came from a hole in the ground on the far side of the field, with a sort of breastwork of sandbags in front.

Here our guide found us again. My section was marched off at right-angles, and after climbing over what seemed to be mounds of loose clay, we were told to move forward along a narrow neck with gaping cavities on either side. The first man negotiated the crossing safely, but when I followed him, one of my feet slid from under me, and I fell over on my back in a hollow full of mud. The weight of my pack held my shoulders down below my body, and it was some time before I could be hauled out, amidst subdued laughter, and managed to climb down into a small sandbag breastwork, where some six of us were crowded.

The men we relieved told us all was quiet and to fire half-right, and then, bidding us good night, filed off into the darkness. A few minutes later

I and another were ordered into another breastwork.  It was only about ten yards away, but we
had to wander round in the mud before we reached
it.  This time we had to cross a small stream by
a bridge of two planks, both broken and sloping
at different angles to the middle.  We landed on
our knees with our feet in the water, and both
thoroughly wet, managed to struggle in and join
two others, who were already in possession.

We made a hot drink as soon as possible and
felt rather better afterwards.  My gum boots had
kept the water out, but I had perspired so much
that the felt lining was quite wet, and they
remained damp and cold until I had an opportunity of drying them some two days later.  It
was beastly cold all night, and I could not feel
my toes at all, but I suddenly discovered a really
good tip.  In the end, kicking sandbags hurts,
and it is much more efficacious to kick the empty
air.  In that way I managed to get some blood
into my toes again.

In the morning we discovered that we were
almost at the point of a right-angle in the line.  In
front of us the ground sloped gently down for
several hundred yards and then rose to a wooded
edge, on which stood a battered château.  On the
right of us, about half as far away, was a small
wood—the "Petit Bois"—which was still held

by the Germans, in spite of an attempt of ours to capture it a few weeks earlier.

The body of a German, at least twice its natural size, lay a short distance in front, and a few others were dotted about the valley, but no living German was to be seen, and it was almost impossible to identify, with any degree of certainty, where their trenches lay. Our own post appeared to consist of a number of small sandbag redoubts, and immediately behind and between was a network of waterlogged holes and trenches, which were quite impassable, and made it impossible to move about from one to another without exposing one's self to the full view of the enemy.

When the sun came out it was quite warm, and the view was as picturesque as one could expect to find in this sad land. We were fairly comfortable, and though there was a certain amount of shelling no shell dropped within fifty yards of us. At nine in the evening we were relieved, and found a billet in a somewhat better farm, near the Creamery, but we lost two men wounded on the way. The following night we marched back to Locre, and ever since then I have been on the semi-sick list with my old complaint, although in all other respects I feel quite fit.

Unfortunately, lice—the War plague—have attacked me at last. I expect it was the hayloft that did it. So far I am not suffering very badly, but when I get warm I am reduced to a condition of wriggling imbecility. Practically every man in the company is in the same condition. I was about the last to succumb. A man in the Worcesters told me that Harrison's Pomade is the only remedy, and I have sent for some. Until I get it I must wriggle.

*22nd February*, 1915.

We returned to our sandbag breastworks on the 14th and had our first taste of real shelling. I was in the same spot as before. For some reason the senior officer in charge wished to annoy the Huns and ordered five rounds of rapid fire at dawn. Of course, we fired at nothing in particular, and except by accident can have done no damage. The Huns apparently thought it necessary to retaliate, but they did it in a saner manner, by shells, not by bullets. They gave us high explosive and large shrapnel right on top of our particular pitch. At first they fell some fifty yards away but crept nearer, until one large shrapnel burst just over our heads and nearly deafened us. One bullet pierced my water-bottle, and, as we had no parados or protection behind us whatever, we decided, on our own responsibility, to move for the time being, to a better bit of trench to our right.

Immediately on our right was a pool of water, ten feet broad, with the bottom of an old tub sticking up in the middle. I made a leap for this, but it turned turtle under me and I had to wade the rest of the way in several feet of water. This mishap was greeted by a shout of laughter, and as soon as I arrived in the trench I had to take off my gum boots and empty them. It was lucky that we moved when we did, as the next big shrapnel exactly caught the breastwork, and when we returned we found a large piece of the shell-case embedded in the sandbag on which I had been leaning. One high explosive fell right inside a traverse close by and wounded twelve men. I was wet through, but as it rained incessantly for two days that did not make much difference.

We returned to our barn that night, but were in again on the following one, this time in the traverse in which we had refuged. It rained incessantly and we had no shelter, but things were quiet. At night when we were relieved I heard something which I never want to hear again. I always thought that the expression "death yell" was a figment of the imagination; but it isn't. Our relief party had arrived and was lined up in the open at the back and above the trench. A flare had shown them to me quite clearly only a few yards away. As it died down a most blood-curdling shriek rang out. It seemed to last for several seconds, falling to a sort of wail, and then ceased. One of the relieving party had been shot clean through the head. He can have felt nothing.

After another night's interval we were in again, and this time for two nights in succession. We heard that some trench had been lost further north and that our reliefs had been sent up to reinforce. The first night I was out with a wiring party. Our wire in front was not very good, and we had to haul into position a number of fresh knife-rests and peg them down. I was one of the carrying party and, until our particular knife-rest was required, we had to hang about at the back of the trench, just about where the man had been shot the night before. Plenty of bullets were flying round, and I lay down as close to the ground as I could get. I don't mind it, when I have something to do, but waiting in the open without cover is not the sort of thing I like.

Apart from bullets things were very quiet. We did no firing at all, and we have since heard that after we were relieved by the Gordons they had a visit from a Hun patrol, anxious to know if the trench was occupied. If the story is true, that patrol did not get back.

We did not get away until 10.30, and when we reached Locre we found our old billet occupied and had to march on to an old barn. I had been more or less wet through for five days and was utterly worn out, but I got a warm drink in the farm kitchen before lying down in the straw.

My hands are in a shocking condition. I have to wear gloves all the time, but the wool sticks to the sore places, and I am not sure that the cure isn't worse than the disease. I don't remember ever having been so tired before, as I was at the beginning of this rest. Luckily the first day we were only paraded once—for rifle inspection. Usually rest is only rest in the Pickwickian sense. In the words of the battalion parody:

> But now I have changed my opinion,
> The name of Rest is a lie, is a lie,
> It is twenty-one rifle inspections
> And forty-eight hours standing by.

There is a large convent here, and I have discovered that baths can be obtained there, a far better thing than to have discovered America. For the first time since I left England I feel really clean.

Yesterday was Sunday, a gorgeous day for a change, and I had a stroll with K. There is a small hill close by with a windmill on the top. They call it Mount Rouge. We wandered up there in the afternoon, and from the platform round the mill we had a wonderful view of the country. They say that on a clear day one can see the sea, but it was too hazy for that; but right up north one could see the towers of Ypres and several other towns, and down south there was a distant ridge, which must have been twenty miles away. Over the Hun lines the country lies as flat as a board to all appearance, until it loses itself in the horizon. The only three hills in the country seem to belong to us. In lieu of tea we had coffee at a cottage by the mill, but they stung us in the price, and the place was as filthy as usual, while the mother of the family was immersed in "La Chasse", over the heads of her children. That appears to be the national sport of Flanders.

At about three one morning there was a great hammering at the barn door, and some of the farm people came in and fetched out a large box. In the morning we heard that the old farmer had died in the night, and the box contained the funeral furnishings, with which the front door is draped when a death occurs in the house. It is the first thing they do.

My Harrison's has arrived, and it seems to be effective, if uncomfortable.

We went back to "F 2"—the trench which smells so badly—on the 22nd. It was very cold, and we had a very dirty march up. The Germans appear to have some fresh troops in the line, for they were panicking away all night, firing volleys every few moments and wasting tons of ammunition to very little purpose. The trench had been much improved since we were last there, but was still unsafe in places, and the night was spent in one long fatigue of sandbag-filling, interspersed with one-hour intervals on guard.

In the daytime there was constant sniping, but the trench was a running stream, well over a foot deep in many places, and we had to turn to and drain it. A sniper caught our platoon sergeant across the back of the neck while he was superintending these operations. I thought he was done for, but we managed to bind him up, and after lying in the trench all day he was carried away by the stretcher-bearers after dark. They say he will live.

When relieved we went back to a farmhouse under Kemmel Hill, and lay in a barn which was comfortable but, I fancy, lousey. The next night we were moved to another barn, where we remained for two days and nights. They shelled the surrounding country pretty freely, and once nearly caught us, for without any warning six shells fell within a few yards, in quick succession, and a number of pieces came through our mud walls. One man had his coat badly torn and seemed to think he was for hospital, but in fact he hadn't got more than a scratch.

Of course, all these barns are what are called "close billets", i.e., one must not move about outside, for fear of being seen and shelled. It follows that one has nothing to do all day, except sleep and eat, but the farm people are generally fairly enterprising and will sell eggs and potatoes at a price. It snowed a good deal, and hot potatoes mixed with margarine, and tinned rabbit highly curried, helped to keep us warm.

I am quite fit again except for my hands and as comfortable as I can expect to be. We are a cheerful lot on the whole, and if one makes up one's mind to have as good a time as possible, it is extraordinary what a lot of little things one can do to increase personal comfort. If a man once starts to be sorry for himself he is finished and done for, and goes down with jaundice or something of that sort in no time. It is curious

how used one can become to even the most
unpleasant details of this life. I don't worry
over much about them myself, and if a man starts
whining about hardships I laugh at him and tell
him that what he is grousing about are mere
discomforts. I really think some of them will end
by believing me. It's the sun which makes the
most difference.

The gentleman with the Cossack cap is an
asset to the company. He is musical and full of
animal spirits. On the march back to rest, when
everyone has had just about enough of life, he sings
us home. Sometimes we feel that it is utterly
impossible to move our leaden feet another step,
but he suddenly strikes up some catching song like
"The Spaniard who Blighted my Life", then a
catch in French: "Connaisez vous le Beau du
Regiment? Il est Mon Amour!", and then perhaps a bit of doggerel of his own composition. It
pulls us together in an amazing manner, and soon
the whole company is singing the old marching
songs and stepping out, as if fatigue were unknown.
I sometimes wonder if we should ever get back
without his assistance. As it is no one falls out.

It is funny to hear "The Lads of the Village"
sung out here. The line, "Facing danger gladly,
where they're needed badly", always comes out
with great gusto and, I fancy, not a little irony.

In the light of the star-shells, within sound of the bullets and half-dead to the world, one doesn't feel much of the gladness, although one may be willing to go on.    Out here I always picture England to myself as a hollow in the hills embosomed in trees, on a sleepy summer day, with an old house in the centre and the call of the rooks overhead. Then it seems as if it may be worth while after all.

Every night, of course, we are all out on fatigue. Sometimes it is a case of a couple of hours only, but in general it means hard work for most of the night.    I am not sure, though, that even these fatigues are not sometimes a blessing.    One trench tour we were only in the line one night, and lying on one's back for three days would become monotonous and is certainly bad for one's condition.

We came out on the 26th and were pleased to find our old billet vacant.    I would sooner lie on a tiled floor than on dirty straw, any day.    They actually gave us six days' rest, instead of four, and, speaking for myself, I enjoyed it.

The first day, four of us lunched at "Emma's" and played bridge all the afternoon.    This time we are not standing by, and on Sunday I got leave and walked with another man into Bailleul, where we had a good meal at the "Canon d'Or", investigated

In Maple Copse, Hooge, June, 1915

[To face page 60

the shops, many more of which are now open, and bought all manner of things for the section, chiefly eatables and domestic utensils. I secured a really ripe piece of Roquefort cheese, which subsequently reposed on the chimneypiece in the billet, just above my head, but I had to look out for reprisals from some of the other occupants. It really was rather strong.

The same evening I had a meal with the Signallers, followed by a concert in their barn. Somehow or other these specialists always manage to make themselves far more comfortable than the ordinary fighting section. It was quite a cheery evening.

The following day we gave a section supper to our section commander. Our billet is an *estaminet* and we hired a room above for the occasion, and ate roast fowl and drank cheap champagne—horrid stuff. We wanted a hare, but our landlord, who fancies himself as a sportsman, could not get one for us. It was just as well, as hares are said to be dirty feeders, and in the present condition of the country I should have had some hesitation about touching one.

They are a curious lot in these Flemish villages. In addition to about fifty soldiers, our billet shelters Monsieur and Madame, three very small children, who have developed measles, a cousin who attends to the customers, and a middle-aged refugee from Messines with his sister.  He is always addressed as *"le vieux Marcheur"*, on account of his somewhat pungent stories.  He is also currently reported to be a spy, but no one interferes with him and he goes and comes as he likes.

It seems spies are as plentiful as blackberries in these parts.  The Huns are said to have a regular tariff for the men in their pay, and up to a couple of months ago, at any rate, these latter used to wander out at night with a rifle and snipe from the trees as our men went up to the line.  No week passes without the sight of some native, his hands roped behind his back, being conducted towards the rear by a file of soldiers.

There is one cottage in Kemmel where we used to gather for coffee.  It had a high chimneypiece, almost as high as the ceiling, and on this, amongst other things, rested a large black teapot.  I heard the other day that the military police had raided the cottage and found, in the teapot, a telephone receiver, the wire from which ran to the Hun lines. I don't know whether this is true, but the cottage is closed.

They say also that dogs are used to carry messages from the villages to the German lines, and some time ago an order was issued that any dog seen near the trenches should be shot.  I myself have seen a small mongrel, once in "F.6", and another time at the back of "F.4". I believe it was shot, in the end.

Everyone throughout the country-side seems to know far more about the movements of the Army than we do ourselves. I was told in our own *estaminet* the other day that in a few days' time there is to be an attack by us, on this part of the front. We know nothing about it ourselves, but a big naval howitzer—known as "Granny" —has been brought up and is in position just outside the village. We have passed it several times on route marches, and it may account for the story.

We have been having a very heavy time—
twelve days in—and for the most part they were
very unpleasant ones. We marched up on the
4th and spent the night in a small barn attached
to a farm at Lindenhoec, in front of Kemmel Hill.
The back of the barn faced the line, and the yard
was sheltered from observation, so we were able
to move about to some extent.

The old farmwife is a great woman. Soup,
*soupe-au-lait,* eggs and hot potatoes are practically
always on tap. An hour or so before we start
for the trenches she is at the barn door, calling
out : " *Œufs pour les trenches,*" " *Oranges pour
les trenches,*" and when we crawl in at two or
three in the morning, she is still up and about,
with a huge cauldron of soup and a basin of
"*pommes de terre tres chauds*". She is making
more money than she ever did before in her life,
I should think, but we thank Heaven for her
existence.

Things in the line itself had got very hot. We
were in the support trench the second night. We
went up the main road amidst bursts of rifle-fire

and were lucky to escape a casualty. One company, coming out by the same road the same night, lost seven men. One poor wretch fell into a shell-hole on the way up and was sent back in charge of another, to dry himself. On his way back he got a bullet in the heart.

We have amongst us a Yorkshireman of mature years. Like me, he finds the carrying rather more than he can comfortably stand. He has a lovely Yorkshire accent which is the joy of the company. One night he was marching up across country a few paces behind me, and for some reason appeared to be even more sorry for himself than usual. All the way up I heard a running commentary from him. " D— t'charcoal," a splash and laughter; " D— t'cooake," another splash and more laughter; " D— t'wetter sheat," a little splash; " D— t'roifle." I don't know whether that went, too, but shortly after there was the biggest splash of all, and amidst a burst of laughter he himself was hauled out of a shell-hole and sent back.

Our guns had been shelling Whaetschaet, the village beyond the ridge, and there was a red glow on the horizon. At times we could see bursts of flame from burning buildings. In the morning there was a lot of shelling from each side. A battery of French 75's shelled the German trenches in front of us, and as our own trench was on the ridge, we could see the explosions quite plainly. The Huns retaliated by shelling the close billets in the rear, and several were set on fire and destroyed.

We came out to our barn that night, but did not reach there until 5 a.m., and at 12.30 the same night went in again. Relieving had become so dangerous and so many casualties had been incurred that it was arranged that, for the future, each company should do forty-eight hours in at a time, instead of the usual twenty-four. The men had rather got the wind up about that open road, and welcomed the change.

Our trench was very little else than a hole in the ground, and what there was of a parapet was partly destroyed the next morning. We all set to work to rebuild and deepen the trench, but we were shelled, off and on, for the whole of the two days, and when we were relieved at 10.30 on the second night we had had about enough for the time being.

On the 11th we were in again after midnight. We tried a new way up across country, instead of by the bullet-swept road. It was not a success. We kept losing touch and got bogged in a swampy field. Finally we had to force a way through a thorn hedge and got rather torn. My tunic was ripped up, and after getting through the hedge I slipped up to my knees in a hole on the far side. The hole proved to be a disused latrine, and for hours after I was an offence to myself and the world.

Immediately we got in, all hands were ordered to start on the work of digging a communication trench down the hill to the front line. We worked right out in the open, in full view of the Huns and with star-shells constantly in the air. It is a matter of constant wonder to me how it is that a working party in such a position is not spotted at once by the enemy. And yet, the only losses we suffered were from chance bullets.

We were told that early in the morning the battalion on our right was to make an attack on the German trenches in front of us, attacking diagonally. Shallow "jumping-off" trenches had been dug on our right a few yards away, and we could see the attacking party gathering in them. The morning dawned in a thick mist, in which very little could be seen, and after a bombardment the attack was postponed until the afternoon. As soon as the mist cleared the Huns spotted the communication trench and shelled it and us heavily.

I spent most of the day hugging a parapet of

wet clay, and with a splitting headache, caused
by a whizzbang which butted into the base of
the parapet against which I happened to be sitting.
At one time the shelling was so heavy and accu-
rate that we were ordered to move down the
trench for a time, and a few moments later a
large woolly-bear shrapnel burst right over our
traverse. When we returned I found that the
spot in which I had been sitting had been well
peppered.

From 2.30 to 4.0 the Huns got something which
sounded very like Hell from our guns. "Granny"
joined in, and her shells passed over our heads
with a roar, rather like the passage of an express
train. We were on higher ground than the
attack and could see all that happened quite
clearly. Bridges had been placed over the front-
line trench, and I watched the attacking party
cross. Our bombardment did not seem to have
done much damage, for, immediately the attack
started, the Hun trenches appeared to be full of
men. One of them got out and sat on his
parapet in spite of our rifle and machine-gun
fire. The attack never had a chance. I watched
the little khaki figures struggle on and fall one
by one. Right in front of them an officer
with his cane. He strolled forward, and from
time to time turned to wave on his men. He

fell not far from the Hun wire, and not more than two or three others, at the outside, got so far. Very few indeed got back.

It was a horrid thing to watch, and it was still more pitiful, the next day, to see the field in front dotted with the bodies of our men. The whole thing was so obviously useless and futile. There must have been at least twenty men in the German trench for every one who attacked. I suppose someone had blundered, as usual.

We ourselves had a good many casualties in the front line, chiefly from machine-gun bullets, which swept the parapet when we were trying to keep down the German fire. Our only casualty in support was our Cossack, who got a bullet in the fleshy part of his arm. I saw him go off to the rear, later, with his face wreathed in smiles, happy in the thought of the blue ticket, which means England again. We shall miss him in the company.

The communication trench was never used, and as it showed up clearly on the slope of the hill it was knocked to pieces in the course of the day.

We stood to all night, expecting a counter-attack which never came, and all the next day they shelled us at intervals, apparently making a special mark of the point where the communication trench joined our own. As this was in our traverse, we had a rather hot time and had to retire down the trench for an hour when it was at its worst. A number of bodies were still lying about in the opposite field, but two or three near the German wire had disappeared during the night, and had apparently been taken in by them.

We were relieved at 2 a.m. next morning, but had trouble getting out. The Huns were very active with their rifles, and we went out by sections. Just as we got to the junction of Oxford Street and Regent Street, i.e., the main Whaetschaet Road, they started volleying, and we lay on our faces in the mud for a good ten minutes, with the bullets whipping the air within inches of our backs. As soon as we could, we got up and doubled up the hill. One man of another section was caught, and as I passed, I saw him lying by the side of the road, with two others binding him up. A star-shell flared at the moment, and in its blue light their faces looked like the faces of ghosts.

Before I got to the top of the hill I was taken with a stitch and could hardly move. One good chap seized my rifle, and with his help I managed to carry on. The "two days in" stunt saves casualties, but is a bit overpowering in its results,

in other ways. We got back to our barn at 4.0,
and I just fell down in the straw and slept until
11.0 in the morning.

It was a gorgeous morning, and after a hefty
meal I felt better. There was a lot of heavy shelling going on to the north. I was placed on billet
guard for some time and watched the big shrapnel
bursting about three miles away. We were to go
out to rest that night, and at 7.30 we packed and
marched out. We only got as far as the road,
a few hundred yards away, however, for there we
were met by a cyclist, and after halting for a few
moments, right-about faced and marched back to
the barn. Heavy fighting was reported at St. Eloi,
just north of us, and our relieving brigade had
been ordered to reinforce. So far as I can make
out, there is very little in the way of troops between
us and the sea.

On the following day—the 15th—we were
told we were to return to the trenches that
night and might be in for some time, but
before we went up we had another little job
to do.

A French 75 battery had been dashing about,
firing from various spots in the neighbourhood,
and in the darkness one of its wagons had wandered into a pond and could not be got out. A
party of us went out to salvage it, without success.

"Y" Wood. Hooge, during the Attack on June 16th, 1915

(From a film found on the body of a soldier killed on that day)

[To face page 72

It was bogged in the mud above the axle-trees, and nothing we could do would move it. Trying to tow a heavy wagon, which one can hardly see in the dark, out of a mire which is equally invisible, is a pretty tough job.

We had a quiet day in the same trench as before. The Huns seemed to have calmed down. Probably they were too much occupied up north. At any rate, they did not trouble us much, and amused themselves, for we distinctly heard a band playing somewhere in their trenches.

It was rumoured that we were to be finally relieved at night, and we waited about with our equipment on for hours. Nothing happened. K and I were sent over to the reserve trench at the top of the hill to gather news, but we could get no information there. A fair number of bullets were hopping around, but nothing out of the common.

It was a misty night, and an hour or so later, in the light of a flare, we saw a party of men on the slope of the ridge, about a hundred yards north of us. For some twenty minutes or more, whenever a flare went up, we saw them still standing there, and came to the conclusion that they were the relieving party for another trench. In the end we sent out a scout to investigate, but just as he was leaving, an officer tumbled into the trench from the rear, and informed us that he was in charge of the relieving party. He had been unable to locate the trench and had left his men in order to investigate. Now he hadn't the slightest idea where to find them. We pointed out the figures in the mist, and they were brought in. They turned out to be a Territorial battalion of a north-country regiment, and had never seen a trench before. They had not the slightest idea that their position on the hill-side was in full view of the Huns, and only one hundred and fifty yards from them, so they hadn't troubled and, luckily enough, were none the worse.

In consequence of the delay we were very late getting out, and after our twelve days in the line, the last thirty-six hours without sleep, we were all fairly done up. The other battalions who were relieved seemed, if anything, in a worse state. All the way to Locre the roadside was dotted with the bodies of their men who had fallen out. At Locre we halted, and to our dismay were told that we must move on to Westoutre, the next village. I sat on the churchyard wall and did not feel as if I could move for the next few hours. Luckily I had reserved a mouthful of rum in my tin bottle, and that started me off again. Someone raised a song, and we sang over the three miles or so, marching into Westoutre, in full strength, at three o'clock in the morning, at a good quick step to the tune of the British Grenadiers. It was really rather a good effort, although the relief at being out of things for a few days is a great tonic.

We have had seven days' rest at Westoutre—
good days, for the most part. Thirty bags of
parcels were waiting for the battalion, so we have
lived on the fat of the land. One of our men had
just had a 21st birthday, and lashings of food had
been sent him, including a bottle of Kümmel. He
himself had retired to hospital, with jaundice or
measles, some days before we came out, so he had
no further use for the tuck. It seemed a pity to
waste it, so on our first evening we had a section
feed on tongue, pork pie, cake, pineapple, pears,
peaches, white wine, and Kümmel. Some feed!

K and I walked over to Locre in the afternoon.
We had all stored a lot of gear in the garret at our
old billet. My gum boots were there and a lot of
other things, which we wanted to retrieve, as we
did not know whether we should see the place
again. We had the walk for nothing, as we found
the village in the occupation of the Canadians. My
gum boots had disappeared, and all our parcels had
been opened and rifled of everything of value which
they contained.

We lay quiet for the next few days, although

some enterprising souls organized a rugger match between our company and another. On the third day, we route-marched to Poperinghe, the only town left to King Albert, except Ypres. We were marched straight through and not allowed to halt or break off, but it was interesting to see a new place.

I am not altogether happy, as my foot gave out on the return and I had to hobble along. I suppose this is the result of all the soaking it has had during the last few months. It gives me the deuce of a time, if I am carrying any weight.

We heard that our sick man was in hospital at Bertin, a few miles to the west, along the ridge which runs from Mount Rouge to Mont des Cats. K and I thought we would try and deliver some of his parcels, so on the Sunday—a lovely spring day—we packed our haversacks full and started off to Bertin along the ridge. We enjoyed the walk, but got nothing from it. At Bertin we were informed that the patient had been evacuated to the base. We handed over most of our stores to the hospital orderlies, reserving enough for our own lunch, and then adjourned to a sunny slope and ate sliced ham, tinned peaches, and chocolate biscuits.

It was a lovely scene below us. Boeschaet lay beneath us, and beyond stretched the flat lands to

Ypres and Poperinghe and right up north to where, I suppose, the Yser was hidden in the mists. It was quite warm. In the middle of our meal, a small girl in her Sunday best came across from a farm on the far side of the field and asked us to come in and have some coffee. We filled her with chocolate biscuits, and after we had finished eating, we walked over to the farm, where we spent half an hour chatting with the family. They were most indignant when I offered to pay for the coffee, much to my surprise. It is the first time I have been given something for nothing in this part of the world, but then, of course, we were actually at the time in France and not in Flanders.

The next day a lot of us had leave to Poperinghe, and K, I and another went over together. It isn't a bad little town, and we had a good lunch at the Restaurante de la Bourse. It was crowded with British and Belgian officers, but we managed to get seats at a table with some Belgians who, judging from the brilliance of their uniforms and decorations, must have been very distinguished individuals. They were quite decent, however, seeing that we were rather dilapidated-looking privates, and questioned us about the battalion and where we had been in the line.

To-day the whole battalion paraded in the rain, for an inspection, and we were told we were to proceed to-night to fresh trenches at St. Eloi, in front of "the Mound", where the recent fighting has taken place. I think we all feel better for the rest. One's nerves get rather jangled up after twelve days in the line, and, although we do not do much actual hard work except in spurts, we are fagged out when our rest starts.

*4th April*, 1915.

I have not been enjoying myself of late. We marched from Westoutre, about nine miles, on *pavé* made greasy by the rain, and in the darkness each foot slipped back an inch or more every time I put it down. We carried two days' rations and heavier packs than ever, and as the result some eighty men fell out on the road. We halted for a few moments at a village called Dickebusche, and then passed on and to the east. At last we reached another village, called Voormezeele, more battered than any I have seen so far. In the light of the star-shells every house appeared to be a ruin.

We wound through this village and mounted a rise. Suddenly out of the darkness in front there loomed up the spectre of a London bus, broken and derelict, but still standing at the side of the road. Here we turned off into the fields, and after jumping several ditches, which gave my foot gip, we crawled through a hole in a hedge, and my own section found itself behind a curved rampart of sandbags about twenty feet long. This so-called trench was only about a foot deep, and there was no protection whatever at the rear and no suggestion of a dugout or other cover.

F

It rained almost constantly for forty-eight hours. There was nothing to sit on except one's pack, and most of the time I sat on that and nursed my foot. Of course, the pack and all its contents were wet through.

When day broke we could see where we were. As usual the ground sloped up in front of us towards the Hun trenches. Behind us, it sloped down to a stream with a row of pollarded willows and then up again to higher wooded ground. Amid the trees on the left, were the ruins of the village we had passed. Just north of us were other ruins —St. Eloi—and in front was something which looked like a spoil heap and which we are told is called "the Mound".

This is the country where the fighting took place a few days ago. The Huns broke right through and some of them reached the Dickebusche Road, but these few retired again, and later most of the lost trenches were recaptured. That we were in, if it could be called a trench, was one of them, but how the dickens we could have expected to hold any line with so little attempt at protection, passes my understanding. They say we may expect an attack at any time.

The second night they took us out and placed us in a support trench at the bottom of the valley. This had only been dug a few days before and, in fact, was not yet completed. It started by the old bus and was known as the "Bus House" trench. It was really a well-made trench, and the first thing we did when we got there was to collect some poles and saplings. There were some sheets of galvanized iron lying about, and with these materials we succeeded in constructing shelters which would at least protect us from the constant rain.

As it happened, the rain stopped and a frost set in. It was bitterly cold, but I took off my boot and, in spite of the pain in my foot, I managed to get some sleep.

Here we spent two days and nights with a hot sun by day and a hard frost by night, and although we had no brazier, we had quite a cushy time, as the enemy left us alone and contented themselves with shelling the ruined village in the rear.

We were relieved on the 27th and marched about five miles to a bit of woodland at the back of Dickebusche, where we sheltered in a number of huts, made of scaffold poles covered by tarpaulins. In the sunshine it was quite a pretty spot, but there was a biting wind from the north, and as my hut opened in that direction, it was almost impossible to keep warm.

My foot utterly gave out. I had to limp all the way down, and when the foot gets at all warm, I

feel it. Owing to the pain I only managed to get
four hours' sleep out of ninety-six. I reported sick
in the morning and the M.O. gave me twenty-four
hours off duty, but the next day the pain was just
as bad, and all he could do for me was to give me
a No. 9 pill. We were going up again that night
and I was ordered to go up "in my own time",
and do the best I could.

Later, however, I was attached to a party of semi-
sick men and, under the charge of two semi-sick
officers, we limped up as far as Voormezeele, where
we were lodged in the cellar of a shattered brewery.
There was not much left of the brewery itself, and
the church, just opposite, showed little but half a
tower. The churchyard was full of gaping holes,
which were not graves, and such of the houses
around as were not mere refuse heaps were roofless
or wall-less. I never saw so complete a picture of
desolation.

We were about six or seven hundred yards from
the firing-line, and every now and then there was
a burst of shrapnel overhead, and some of the
bullets found the entrance to our cellar, re-
bounded to the roof, and then played around
the room.

There was nothing to do all day but to lie on
one's back or cook hot drinks in a sheltered corner
of the courtyard. Apart from my foot, I felt

particularly hearty. Once or twice, when no shelling was on, I wandered about the village, keeping under shelter, and in one cottage garden I found a clump of spring violets. It is curious how pleased one can be with a little thing like that, and how it bucks one up.

After two days in the cellar, we limped back to the wood and I paid another visit to the M.O. He told me he could do nothing for me except in the way of a No. 9, so I decided to cut him out and carry on as well as I could. They don't send one to the Base with rheumatism, unless one is very bad indeed, and to be sick or semi-sick at the front is a rotten job. Wounded, one is in clover, but for a sick man the Army has no use whatever.

After a day in the wood, where we were nearly frozen, we were moved into billets in Dickebusche village. My company is billeted all together, in a large *estaminet*. A narrow staircase leads to the first floor, and a still narrower one from there to the floor above. My platoon and one other carpet the first floor, and the rest go up above. If we had to get out in a hurry, there would be trouble, for only one man can descend at once. Apart from that I am more comfortable than at any time since I came out. There is a wooden floor and one is both warm and dry.

Last night several hundred of us were ordered on fatigue to dig trenches. We started with spades and rifles, but it began to rain in torrents, and after going a mile, we were ordered back again, wet through. We go up to the line again to-night.

We marched up again on the 4th, but this time to a much better trench, "P 2", two hundred yards or so to the south of our breastwork. We went up by a different route, across country for the most part, and it took it out of my foot pretty badly. As a finishing touch, as soon as we got in, I was ordered with K on listening post. This meant crouching on one's toes in six inches of mud, behind a small mound of clay, just outside the end of the trench, and watching a hedge and ditch which led up towards the German lines. I was there for an hour, and as I had to keep my toes bent the whole time, my foot gave me no peace, and at the end of my watch I had to be helped over the parapet into the trench.

When we got in, we reported to the Captain, and after inspecting the post, he came to the conclusion that it was quite useless, and it was promptly washed out. It rained for the greater part of the next forty-eight hours and we were without any shelter in our traverse, as the only dugout had been appropriated by the machine-gun section, who held a post at the end.

The whole trench is enfiladed from the Mound, and unless one keeps very low down one is likely to be caught by a Hun sniper. The trench itself stinks. There are no latrines and I should think there must be bodies in the parados.

Apart from the weather, we were left more or less in peace, but we were all wet through when we were relieved at 2 a.m. on the third night. We spent the next two days in the cellars of the Château of Elzenwalle, which lay just beyond the ridge at the back of the valley. The Château has been torn to pieces by shells, and everything above the ground floor is in a dangerous condition, and might collapse at any time. Even the cellars have holes in them, and they smell like a cesspool. We did our best to drown the smell in chloride of lime, but it nearly made one sick. Still, it is better than the open trench in such weather.

One of the two nights I went on fatigue carrying planks to the trenches. On the soft ground my foot is not so bad, but we had to jump about thirty ditches each way and I can't do that with comfort. We were relieved on the 8th, and owing to the condition of my foot, I got leave to come on in advance of the company. I was lucky enough to run across the mess cart of another battalion. They gave me a lift, but it was an uncomfortable conveyance and I was shaken to pieces.

Communication Trench, Sanctuary Wood, June, 1915

[To face page 88

As soon as I got in, I hobbled out and bought two bottles of white wine, a tin of peaches, and some oranges and biscuits, for the delectation of the section when it marched in, and we managed quite a cheery meal.

The Powers have served us out special green envelopes for letters. These will not be censored except, possibly, at the Base, and the writer has to certify thereon that he is not giving away information which might be useful to the enemy. This is a new stunt, and one will be able in the future to write home without the knowledge that all one says will be read by one of the Company officers.

One lives here in a way which upsets all one's old ideas of life. One does things without a qualm —latrine fatigue, for example—which would have made one physically sick in England. One seems absolutely cut off from all the decent ideas of civilization, and a letter from home is the only connecting thread. Fancy feeling really clean once more, and free from vermin. As soon as we came out last time, I washed all over in cold water, but it had to be done in full view of the public.

The last two nights we have all been out on fatigue. The first, we marched to the trenches with spades, four miles each way, and dug a support trench behind the firing-line. If one has to do that in the open with bullets flying round, it is astonishing how soon one can make a respectable hole in the ground. The great thing is to make some sort of head cover in the shortest possible time. It was pretty heavy work and we were not back until 3.30 a.m.

The second night we carried coils of barbed wire up to a new redoubt in the wood, just at the back of our last trench. It was very dark, and going across country I managed to lose touch with the man in front. I succeeded in finding my own way, however. We go in for five days again to-night.

We have been having a more exciting time than usual. The Huns have been particularly busy, firing volleys at the parapet all night long. They are really the most lively tribe we have come across. The night we got in, a Zeppelin sailed right down the line above our heads. I could hear it long before I knew what it was, for it was difficult to distinguish in the darkness. Our anti-aircraft guns were firing at it for a long time, but apparently did no damage. I hear that it dropped bombs on some villages farther south and wrecked a house or two, but it attempted nothing on the trenches, although it was quite low down.

The following day they shelled us during the afternoon, but our own trench escaped, although for the time being we had to move down from one end. Our own guns are usually silent. They say they are only allowed to fire three rounds per day, as ammunition is very short. The idea makes one rather wild.

We spent all the night on fatigue. I personally filled thirty sandbags at the back of the trench, and carried them in, for raising the parapet and

traverses to protect us from the Mound snipers.
For half an hour about midnight I was out in front,
carrying and pegging down knife rests to cover a
gap in the line. We carried them to a vacant spot
between our trench and the next and about fifty
yards from the Huns. They were doing a lot of
firing, and as we were right out in the open, the
situation was not without its charms, for those who
like that sort of thing. It was much preferable,
in any case, to my last experience of that sort of
work, but I don't pretend to be a fire-eater, and
I am not fond of wandering about in front with
the bullets flying, and bobbing down whenever a
flare rises. One feels very large and lonely and
unclothed under those circumstances. About
twenty of us were out, but no one was hurt.

The weather was fine, warm, and sunny. Our
particular trench, "P2", ends in a bit of woodland
with a number of large trees, and it would be quite
a pretty scene in other times. Unluckily, there are
several dead cows lying about, and with the warmer
weather they are getting rather lively, especially
when the wind comes from their direction. My
suspicions of the parados also seem to be justified.
Our predecessors attempted to rebuild it at one spot,
but finding a number of corpses inside, had to
abandon the attempt.

On the 14th I had rather a narrow shave and

nearly got a blue ticket. I was holding up a trench periscope, while K looked through it with a pair of field-glasses. I had turned away for a moment when I suddenly felt a smart blow on the upper part of the arm. I thought I was wounded at first and asked K to look. At the back of the arm, deeply embedded in my greatcoat, he found a bullet. It was splayed out and must have come clean through a weak spot in the parapet. It will be quite useful as a souvenir.

We were relieved by another Company about ten that night and went back to the Château. We were just entering the gate when there was a loud explosion and a big rifle fire broke out, followed within a minute or two by all our own batteries. We stood to for a time, but after half an hour things became quiet again. It appears that the Huns exploded a mine under an advanced trench and then sent over a lot of shrapnel.

My foot has been sometimes rather better. The weather has been much warmer and drier, and I hope the foot will improve with it. I sat in the sun most of that day, and fished in the Château moat with a stick, a bit of thread, a bent pin, and a worm. I didn't catch anything, not even a stickleback, and I don't think I ever expected to, but if I had only had a stone jar by my side, I should have felt the "compleat angler".

There are piles of torn papers in the cellars, and one day I picked up a picture post card, which rather interested me. It was addressed to Madame de ———, the Châtelaine of Elzenwalle, from Ridgway Place, Wimbledon. I suppose the lady is English, or has English connections. I am sorry for her, when she sees her home again, though.

On our return to the firing-line, we went into the breastworks, which we held when we first arrived. We had rather a warm time, for they absolutely pelted the parapet with bullets for many hours. About 2.30 a.m. the row ceased, and for at least an hour after not a bullet was fired, and not a single star-shell went up. We could hear the Huns working, and we all stood to in readiness for an attack until after dawn, but nothing happened.

The day was beautiful and very quiet. Half of us slept in the sun behind the breastwork. With the evening, however, came rain and the darkest of nights. It was so dark that the relief took four hours to come up, and we had to feel our own way back a step at a time. My foot caught me again after an interval of some days, and I was in a pretty wretched condition.

On the 17th K and I got leave and walked into Ypres. Blocks of houses in the town have been destroyed, but most of it is untouched so far. We had a good lunch at a restaurant in the Grand Place near the Cloth Hall, and strolled round the town. There was a bit of a market on and crowds of people were about. We went into the cathedral. A shell had come through the roof and the choir stalls were a mass of rubbish. Most of the windows were smashed, and we looked about for some of the old stained glass, but without success. I believe there was some rather fine glass somewhere there.

The Cloth Hall has lost its roof, and the frescoes are ruined, but they were not of any antiquity.

After we got back to our billet at Dickebusche, a fierce cannonade broke out, and the old town seemed to be getting the full benefit of it. I hear there was trouble a little to the south of the town, where we are said to have made a successful attack.

As half the battalion has been standing by during this rest, we have had a much easier time of it. The troops cannot go on fatigue if they must be ready to turn out to reinforce at fifteen minutes' notice.

Our principal meal is breakfast. My section have annexed a particular *estaminet*, where Madame is very obliging, at a price. I am mess secretary, so I go out a few minutes earlier in the morning, and search for eggs and anything else that happens to be going, on my way down the street. Yesterday, breakfast consisted of eggs, sausages, liver and kidneys, with bacon, jam and bread from the rations. The price of the meal worked out, with the cooking, at 8d. per head. One does not want much more for the rest of the day and can subsist quite well on Army rations.

When I first came out, biscuits, jam, and bully beef were about all the rations we received. Nowadays, we get tinned butter or margarine, real bread and cooked meat and bacon for breakfast. Another thing I buy, when I can, is onions, and these I take with me to the trenches. The section was very scornful at first and sniffed audibly. Now they want to eat my onions, and one or two of the bolder sort even purchase for themselves.

The local Flemings are not nice people. If they could only choose, I am sure they would prefer the Huns to ourselves. One of our men went into a shop, and after buying forty francs' worth of stuff, the woman tried to do him over the price. He objected. *"Anglais soldat no bon, Alleman bon,"* she said. If the positions had been reversed, I rather wonder what would have happened to her.

The section is in a bad way. Last time we were up, there were only five of us. Three have gone down with jaundice, pleurisy, and piles, and several

The Great Crater at Hooge

[To face page 96

of the remainder are far from fit. Apart from my
foot, I keep wonderfully well and have learnt to
take care of myself. Lanoline cured my hands,
and frequent dressings of Harrison's Pomade keep
down a "certain liveliness". Luckily I don't suffer
in that way so badly as many of us do. To some
extent, also, one has learnt what to carry, or rather
what not to carry. A single piece of soap lasts for
ever, when one can only wash three days in the
week, and with the warmer weather one does not
need woollens. I discarded my goatskin some time
ago, but one likes a spare shirt and vest. Someone
sent me out a beautiful vest, soft and lined with a
sort of cotton wool, but it turned out to be a regular
nest for vermin. I received a shirt also, but the
good lady who made it had either run short of
material, or had forgotten the tails entirely. At
any rate, it only reached to the waist.

The latest stunt is bombing. A new sort of
bomb, more substantial than the jam-pot brand, has
been produced. Bomber volunteers have been
called for, and practice goes on daily at the back
of the village. So far very few men in the Army
seem to know much about these things. The story
goes that an Irish battalion, which was holding a
trench, not more than twenty-five yards from the
enemy, had these new bombs served out to them.
On the next night they threw two hundred of them

G

into the Hun trench. Afterwards, the Huns pulled out the detonators and threw them all back, to the discomfiture of the Irish.

Another really good stunt has just been started. There is a large brasserie just outside the village. It isn't working, and has been converted into a bathing establishment. The troops are marched down by detachments, and each man can have a large tub, into which he can curl the whole of his body. I had a turn there myself yesterday and splashed about to my heart's content.

After I had bathed, I turned into the battalion shoemakers' shop to have my boots mended, and was waiting there when without any warning a large shell burst about a hundred yards away, followed by a number of others, all close together. One large house was wrecked, and all the troops streamed out of the village towards the rear, together with the inhabitants. I saw two of our men carrying an old woman, but though they ran, everyone seemed to take things quite calmly, and after a dozen rounds or so, the shelling stopped. We could see the shells falling into Ypres most of the day, and I believe they are having a very bad time there.

The weather has been beautiful, and I spent the afternoon after the shelling lying on my back in a field. There is, of course, another side to the picture. The longer the day, the more time for shelling, and the hotter the sun, the more need of chloride of lime. My feet are shockingly tender, but I can manage to walk all right. We were out trench-digging until midnight and they did not trouble me overmuch.

*28th April*, 1915.

We went up for four days on the 20th, and in some ways we had a quiet time. Heavy fighting was going on at Hill 60 just to the north of our part of the line, and the guns pounded away all day and all night. We spent three days in the front line and rather expected an attack that never came off.

On the first day we lost our section commander, shot in the arm, and the next day the Company Sergeant-Major was shot dead by a sniper from the Mound while he was directing some fatigue at the back of the trench.

The same afternoon we had rather a curious experience. Without any obvious reason, everyone's eyes began to smart, until the tears ran down one's cheeks. We heard by telephone that the men in the support line were suffering in the same way. There was no smell or any other natural cause for it, and after a quarter of an hour the worst of it passed off. The Captain came round and told us it was said to be the effect of brick dust, driven down-wind, from the burning of Ypres. It was only when we came out that we found that the

Huns had been discharging gas north of Ypres. The gas was practically dissipated before it reached us, but there seems to have been serious trouble with it in the north.

The third evening they started throwing rifle- and hand-grenades at our trench, our first experience of such things. Nearly all of them fell short, but one landed on the parapet and wounded three men slightly. That night we went back to the Bus House trench in support. One can sleep there, but I had to take off my boots for a couple of hours before I could get off. Luckily, although very tender, my foot stood the marching better than usual.

We were relieved the next night and marched back to Dickebusche in the light of burning Ypres. I could see the towers standing out black against the red flames. The town must be about finished. Our casualties during the four days were thirty, rather heavy for us, but most of them were slight.

This life is a very different thing in these hot quiet days from what it was in the winter. I find carrying easier than I did, and I am not always cold and wet through. I don't think I shall ever forget the curious, unreal peace of the nights. One has a sort of quiet enjoyment in them and one can't realize, or even remember, except subconsciously, I suppose, that any moment may be one's last.

We always go up the same way now, past the church, over the causeway by the lake, and then up a rising cart road through the wood. Once past that, we are in the danger zone and bullets buzz by occasionally. A couple of hundred yards beyond, we come to a corner where stands an abandoned brasserie, now the Headquarters of the battalion we are relieving. Round the corner, another quarter of a mile, brings us to a point where the road is blocked by two breastworks of sandbags ten feet high and overlapping in the middle. Here is a sentry post, and the order is passed down: " Single file, and quick past the barrier." We file past and go on at the double, for just at this spot we have already lost several of our best men.

Another two hundred yards and we turn off into the fields on our right and find ourselves on the crest, above a shallow valley. On the opposite side are the Hun lines, and down below the loom of trees makes a darker patch in the darkness. There is a young moon and the stars are brilliant, so that one can see without fear of being seen. We pass on down the slope. Suddenly there is a rattle of rifle-fire, taking the place of the one shot per minute which is the usual average. A star-shell flares out, followed by six others, and the whole valley is lighted up. One feels very visible, although one knows perfectly well that one cannot be seen.

Someone mutters: "The Huns are grumpy to-night." The firing dies down again, but as we approach the wood, the single shots take on a new sharp note, as the bullets strike the twigs. It gives them a curious metallic sound. We pass a stretcher-party carrying a motionless form, and under the wood are two men, kneeling over a third, whose thigh is covered by a dark stained bandage. Some-one whispers: "Who is it?" and the reply tells us that it is one of ourselves. With the man on the stretcher, he forms the harvest of that little burst of fire a few moments before. He bled to death before they could get him to the dressing-station.

We cross the stream by a plank bridge and are challenged by a low voice out of the darkness: "Who goes there?" We pass the end of the Bus House trench, winding through the barbed wire which protects it in front, and begin to climb the hill. Here we are more or less safe from bullets from the front, but now and again one from the left buries itself in the earth at our feet or hisses by, just over our heads.

In front looms a row of small trees and the relics of a hedge, and we know that we have reached our trench safely. We file in through an opening in the parados and turn to the left, crushing past the men, who stand in full equipment, ready to leave for rest, as soon as we have taken over from them. We wind in and out around the traverses, sometimes between walls of sandbags eight feet high, sometimes bending double where the parapet is lower. " Cheer-o, Wilts." " Cheer-o, H.A.C." " What sort of luck?" " Oh, a quiet time, three wounded. Keep down by the dugout, the bullets come through there. Had one man hit already. Keep a good look out. The Huns may attack, they have removed some of their wire. We have had two men out in front, and they say the Huns have sapped half-way across. Good night. Good luck." " Good night. Have a good rest."

We settle ourselves in our traverse, which is right at the extreme end of the trench, and occupy our dugout. The section commander orders K and me on guard at once, one at each end of the traverse. I throw off my pack, fix my bayonet, slip a cartridge in the chamber of my rifle, and retire to the end of the traverse, where I stand on the firing-step and peer into the night.

It is too dark to see anything clearly at first, particularly dark under the hedge which runs up to the German lines, just in front of me. Is that a movement in front? That dark figure? No, only a post in the wire. Against the skyline are the Hun trenches, one hundred and fifty yards away. In the middle of the field is something

which, in the darkness, looks like the scaffolding
of a travelling crane. In reality, I know that it
is a row of sloping hop poles, joined together at
the top.

A spurt of flame on the skyline and my head
ducks in a hurry. I cannot keep it up for long,
for the bullets pound into the parapet, and although
I know that I cannot be seen, a chance bullet is
as bad as any other.

A star-shell goes up on the left. Up goes my
head again only to be withdrawn as it falls, a few
seconds before the hail of lead which follows it.
" Where's old ——?" says a voice. " On guard,"
is the reply. " A hot gripe's going—like some?"
Someone hands me a tin cup of cocoa. K's voice
in the darkness: " Can you hear anything?"
" No." " A sort of tapping seems to come from
the hedge. Put a bullet down it." We both fire
one or two shots down the hedge, and another at
a point from which a Hun appears to be firing,
but as the sight on one's rifle is invisible even to
oneself, the aim is pure guesswork.

Suddenly I see something black on the parapet.
I aim. A Hun? No, only a rat. An hour has
passed and my guard is over. I sit down in a
dugout for a moment, but almost at once I am
called out to fill sandbags. We go out at the back
of the trench with spades and bags and start work.

A bullet comes along occasionally, but no one is hit. Suddenly the distant rifle-fire in the north becomes louder and nearer. " More panicking," says someone. Instead of being confused and sporadic, the fire seems to come in rolls. An order is given : " All stand to." We rush back into the trench, to our own traverse, and with rifle in hand or within reach, wait for the attack which never seems to come.

Half an hour passes and the firing dies down. Back we go to our sandbag-filling, until it is time for me to go on guard again. Then I take up my old position, and for an hour watch the Hun lines, the dark hedge, and the brilliant stars, wondering what they are doing at home, and wishing I were in a comfortable bed again. I see a light in the Hun trenches. Something like a rocket starts to rise, but falls to the ground within a few yards. " Look out, grenade coming." A few seconds later there is a dull boom in front of the parapet. The grenade has fallen short.

During the next quarter of an hour we get several of them, but no damage is done. From time to time during the night, news comes through on the telephone. We learn that we had five casualties in the relief and that so and so of such a company has gone west. All night long the big guns pound away in the north and a red glare lights up the

northern horizon.    At 3.30 the dawn begins to
break, and we stand to again until it is broad
daylight.

In the daytime, except for the men on guard,
who watch through periscopes, there is nothing to
be done.   We eat or lie up in a dugout or on the
fire-step, or even, when it is dry, in the bottom of
the trench.   One can see nothing in front, for it
is death to get one's head above the parapet, but
the view to the rear over the parados is unimpeded.
In the sunlight it is picturesque to a degree.   The
grass in the field below us has grown waist high,
and hides the bodies of animals, which were to be
seen a few weeks ago.   There are big patches of
yellow, where last year's turnips have flowered.

The ruins of the village are half-hidden by trees,
and the hills are crowned by woods.    At its
southern end our trench runs into a little patch of
woodland, with forest trees, amongst whose roots
dugouts have been formed, and through it runs a
stream.   We used to boil its water for drinking,
but it comes from the Hun lines and is said to
have been poisoned.   I don't believe that story
myself, for I walked down a communication trench
and had a very satisfactory wash, without any
harmful result.   The men we relieved suffered from
some skin complaint, which they attributed to the
water.   Anyway, it did me good, for I am a thirsty

The Menin Road, September, 1915

[To face page 108

soul, and in this hot weather one bottle of water a day does not go very far with me. A good wash helps no end.

I am getting sick of fatigues. Each night since we came out to rest we have had to march out to the trenches carrying something or other, and we are so short of men that when a fatigue is ordered every available man in the battalion has to go. To-night we go again.

This time our rest has been more exciting than the line. Yesterday an order was issued that if the Huns started to shell the village all the men were to leave the billets at once and rally in the rear, near the wood where we first rested here. A new draft had arrived on the 26th, and about 7 p.m. that day, I was talking to a signaller in the street, when a big shrapnel shell burst right above us. We flung ourselves instinctively against the wall and then dashed into the side entrance of our billet for our rifles. Just inside we met the Captain. " Out with you," he cried, and without rifles or equipment we dashed across the road and over the fields at the rear.

I was right in the middle of the first field when I heard another shell coming. I saw three burst at once high overhead and about seventy yards behind us. I threw myself flat on the ground at once. The bullets cut up the ground all around me and for thirty yards in front. When the next round came I managed to fall in a ditch, and after that I got out of range. One couldn't help laughing at the sights. The whole country-side was dotted with men, women, and children, and horses, a number of which had stampeded, and the appearance of some of them, particularly the civvies, was very funny.

We lost over twenty men, most of them from the new draft which had just arrived, but only a few were killed. Two or three civvies were killed and a few wounded. We paraded near the wood, some of us without rifles, much to the Colonel's indignation.

We had to go up on fatigue afterwards, carrying knife-rests, and they were shelling the road on either side. I have never before seen it so lively at night.

Yesterday we got it again about noon, but this time succeeded in retiring in something like order. Our billet was a regular death-trap, and one shell might have wiped out the whole company, so at 5.0 in the afternoon we left it, and took up our quarters at an isolated farm about a quarter of a mile from the village.

Almost before we had settled in they started to shell both the village and the main road with what are said to be armour-piercing shells from an

Austrian naval gun. One can't hear them coming, and if they strike the soft ground, they make a hole about eighteen inches wide, but don't explode. They all came from the north, and at first we thought they were duds.

Our new farm is regarded as a close billet, as it can be seen from the Hun lines, so we are not allowed outside. Inside we have only one barn, so the space is a bit congested.

We went up again to "P.2" on the 28th and had two gorgeous days, regular summer days, and very quiet ones, although there were one or two heavy bombardments in the north. One man had his hair parted by a bullet which just grazed the scalp, and another received, full on his head, a grenade, which did not explode, but merely knocked him out for the time being. So far as I can hear we only had two serious casualties.

The most unpleasant things were the flies, great yellow things, which swarmed all over the place. As a result we had to go out at night and bury such carcasses as we could get at.

We were told that the Huns were supposed to have mined under the trench, and were ordered to listen for sounds by poking a stick into the ground and placing one's ear to the upper end. I never succeeded in hearing anything that way myself, but the idea that one may be blown sky-high at any moment is not altogether a pleasant one.

We had another gorgeous two days in reserve in a wood known as Ridgewood, under tarpaulin tents. A good many shells fell on each side of us, but they left the wood untouched, and it was quite a picnic and very pleasant after some of our experiences.

When we left the wood we came back to rest at a new farm a few hundred yards from the last one, which had been shelled and partly destroyed since we left. An Irish battalion had taken it over from us, but as they insisted on spreading themselves about in the open, they were seen, with the usual result.

Our new farm is a much better billet, as we have a large loft floored with tiles, but during the last few days the farm folk have been carting away the mess which usually fills the yard of a Flemish farm, and the smell is enough to knock one down. I think that the farm itself must be built on the site of an old château. It is surrounded by a dirty moat, and there is a fine avenue as an approach and some relic of a bridge with big gates, but the building itself is fairly new.

The night after we got here, two hundred of us were dragged out to dig a communication trench at the top of the ridge, and we were unlucky enough to have five casualties.

K and I got leave to go into Locre the other day. We got a lift there in a lorry, but the road was crowded with refugees flying from the north. There must have been hundreds of carts and barrows piled with household goods, all making for the French frontier.

I have received a parcel of fifty gas respirators, little pads to tie over the mouth and nose. I believe the Army is issuing them, but the official supply has not yet arrived. They are entirely useless unless damp, and we are instructed in case of need to damp them in any way possible.

For the last two days we have been standing by. They say the Huns have recaptured Hill 60, and we are to be ready to reinforce if required. I have spent most of the time lying on my back by the moat or playing the game of *vingt-et-un*, without much profit to myself. We go back to Ridgewood to-night.

21*st* *May*, 1915.

We spent five days in Ridgewood in reserve. The weather was fine and hot and we played cricket at the back of the wood. The Engineers have built two rows of trenches right through the wood, and in place of our tents we have roofed over alternate traverses in the rear trench, for use as dugouts, which are both roomy and comfortable. We had to fetch up some old light railway lines, stacks of which were available near the lake, and these were covered with galvanized iron and sandbags, giving absolute protection except against a direct hit.

The last night in the wood I was on guard and found it bitterly cold. I think I must have got a bad chill or a touch of influenza. We went up to the support trench the next evening, and there I found a good dugout, but all night I felt very ill, with pains all over me. After two days we moved up to an advanced trench, which was, on the whole, the very worst I have ever been in. It was merely a low sandbag breastwork with no shelter. I was very sick as soon as I arrived there, and to make matters worse, the weather changed

117

and it rained hard. I could not find a dry spot where I could stretch myself out, so I sat and shivered, with my teeth chattering, for about thirty hours. I was so fed up that I managed to get detailed for water fatigue the second night. We went down through a new communication trench in the wood, but it was about a foot deep in water, so I was wetter than ever when I got back.

We were so near the Huns that it was dangerous for them to shell us, and they did not worry us with grenades as usual. After two days of rain the sun came out again, and we managed to. get dry, but by that time I was pretty well done in. The officer in charge ordered me into his dugout, where I slept for a couple of hours.

We marched out to the brasserie that night and there I slept on the ground under the entrance-gate. It rained again, and by the time we reached our farm in the evening we were wet through again. In the dark we lost our way and had to cross a fair-sized stream by a bridge of a slippery tree-trunk. For a wonder, I negotiated it safely, but several men fell into the stream and had to be fished out.

I was as weak as a rat and began to feel that I was too old for this sort of life. Nowadays it is one continuous fatigue when one isn't in the line. One day there was a fatigue in the afternoon to the transport field, two miles away, for water, and the same night there was another to the trenches. Another man, knowing my condition, offered to take my place at night, so I escaped. The next day I was on billet guard all day, and at night there was another fatigue to the trenches, but it rained so hard that this was cancelled. I am feeling rather better now, but not very strong.

The Huns put a few shells into the village every day, and one day shelled our H.Q., but the trenches themselves are more quiet than usual. The village has been abandoned and we cannot buy food there as we used to. The great shop, "Lipton", as we called it, has moved to another village. This is rather unfortunate, as for some reason or other rations have been very short of late, and for a time we had not enough to eat as our parcels from home had not arrived.

I have been trying to unearth the origin of a word by which the Army designates the local inhabitants. I don't know how it is spelt, but it sounds like "Gonzoubri". Everyone uses it, but no one seems to know why, although there is a story that it was the invention of a company cook, to describe the gangs of labourers, who have been recruited locally by the Belgian Government, for trench digging. They look rather like brigands and might be called anything, but the explanation does not explain.

The little pad respirators are now said to be practically useless against gas, and they are issuing cloth caps with talc eyepieces. These are drawn down over the head and tucked into the tunic below.

The weather is hot again and most of the mud has dried up, so although we go up again to-night, I shall not feel as I did last time.

4*th June*, 1915.

We have been having fine weather and rather an interesting time. We spent four days in moderate comfort in the support trench. Behind us was a network of little trenches, leading to rubbish tips, latrines, and the stream. Here it flows between high banks, and one can go down and wash, even in daylight, without being seen. Apart from a shell screaming overhead now and then, an occasional rifle-shot, and the sound of distant guns, everything was very peaceful.

The first day they shelled us a bit, but did no damage, and after that they left us alone. Two nights we were out digging fresh trenches behind the firing-line, and another we were carrying up corrugated iron and knife-rests. I was rather amused over the digging. With one of the last few drafts there arrived two boys, who should be twins. They are quite good boys, but perfect little gentlemen on all occasions. On this occasion they had each built up a portion of the parapet in the new trench, and I overheard them inspecting each other's work. Each swore that the other's work was better than his own. Each asserted that the other's sandbags were better filled and more symmetrical than his own. I really thought that they would end by quarrelling on the subject.

We were digging on that occasion until two o'clock in the morning. After we got back, I went to sleep in a dugout, but an hour later was aroused by someone shaking me, and asking if I had got my respirator. I found a shocking smell of gas outside, and judging by the row, a big fight was going on to the north of us. Luckily, by the time it reached us, the gas was not strong enough to do much harm. We all stood to and watched the shrapnel bursting a mile or so away. I saw the twins helping each other with their respirators, and a few hours later they were sleeping in the sun, in the bottom of the trench, wrapped in each other's arms.

Later in the day I overheard another conversation between them. They always use the editorial We. Said one to the other: " We have to thank you for that good curry." Then came the reply : " Oh, but we had to thank you for the hot gripe last night."

Our chief interest in the daytime is watching the planes. I have seen two Huns brought down, and they seem to have been driven off the sky. One ventured over our lines the other day, but in about four minutes he had had enough, and retired

Front-Line Trench, Sanctuary Wood, near Hooge, July, 1915

*[To face page* 122

surrounded by over a hundred puffs of shrapnel. Our own planes seem to wander round as if quite indifferent to the guns.

After five days we moved to our dugouts in the wood. They are really quite comfortable, and one does not catch things there, as one does in these barns. It was very hot and we were eaten up by mosquitoes. One man had a head almost twice its natural size, and I had three huge lumps on my face. Most of us look like gipsies, from the heat.

After four days in the wood we had four more days in the front line in "P.2". We had nine casualties going up, and when we arrived were told that the Huns were massing in front of us in preparation for an attack. It was hotter than ever, and the stench sometimes was awful. Luckily the wind blew chiefly from the rear, although an undercurrent, particularly at night, from the opposite direction, seemed to have found some especially undesirable corpse.

Each day we had some little excitement. The first night some houses at St. Eloi caught fire. There must have been some explosive stored there, and one of them either exploded or fell in, sending a column of smoke and flame at least a hundred feet into the air. The second night at sunset, a Zeppelin passed over Ypres from east to west. I

suppose this was one of the fleet that raided London
that night, but of course we knew nothing of this
at the time.    The third night a fleet of planes
crossed our lines just before dawn.   We heard six
or eight of them, but could see nothing, and as
we had never heard them before at such an hour,
we were rather curious.

The fourth day was the best.    About noon
everything was very quiet, except for an occasional
shot, when without any warning a furious fire burst
out from the Hun lines a little to our left.   We
jumped for our rifles and had manned the parapet
within four seconds, even a man who was sleeping
in a dugout.    The firing lasted for about five
minutes and then ceased as suddenly as it began.
Immediately after, the Huns gave a big cheer, and
all was quiet again.   I fancy it was only an attempt
to wake us up a bit, but they may have been
celebrating the raid on London, of which we heard
a rumour that evening.

That night we were relieved, but not until 1.0
in the morning.   A lot of firing was going on at
the time, so we took advantage of a communication
trench, which had just been finished.   It was about
half a mile long and ended beyond the barricade
near the brasserie.   It was the first time we had
used a communication trench of this nature, and
we did not care for it much.   It was very slow

going, and as we were not to rest at Dickebusche,
but were to move a couple of miles farther on, it
was 4.0 a.m. before we reached our destination.

This turned out to be an open field. It started
to drizzle just as I lay down to sleep, but it didn't
last long and I slept like a top, until 9.0 in the
morning. I found a farm close by and a great
number of women were hanging about, with
baskets of eggs, butter, oranges, and chocolate. I
bought some eggs, milk from the farm, and butter,
and breakfasted, and after having shaved and per-
formed very public ablutions, I tried to sleep again,
but found the sun too hot.

There appeared to be troops everywhere. Each
of the surrounding fields was occupied, and at least
half a dozen battalions passed our field during the
day. It is rumoured that the division is to hold
the tip of the Salient and that we move into Ypres
at once. Personally, I should not mind how long
we stayed where we are. It is lovely weather and
decent country, and the farmhouses have no holes
in their roofs or sides.

We marched into Ypres on the 4th, a four-mile march in the heat of the day. All the inhabitants have been evacuated and the town is deserted except for troops. We entered by the Lille Gate, and turning right, inside the ramparts, were stored in enormous cellars, not far from the Menin Gate. These cellars are inside the ramparts themselves, but appear to be immensely strong and can easily accommodate the whole battalion.

I was placed on gas and aeroplane guard in front of the cellars at once, so I had no opportunity to investigate. At regular intervals shells fell into the town, and that first night we had seven casualties.

We had relieved the Life Guards, who were doing dismounted duty, and before leaving they told us that there was much wine in the town. As usual the machine-gunners found it. Close by the cellars was an open space with the remains of a church in the centre. A high-walled garden abutted on this space. One glance through the broken wall showed a shell-hole amid a mass of broken bottles in the garden. The owner had evidently buried his wine, and although the shell had destroyed much, many hundreds of bottles still remained. That afternoon the battalion drank and made merry, and when at 8.0 p.m. four hundred and thirty men were ordered on fatigue, many of them were not in the best of condition.

Two hundred and fifteen knife-rests had to be carried up to Maple Copse, and the procession was over a mile long. We picked them up in a field just outside the Lille Gate about 9.0, but it must have been 10.0 o'clock before the last of us got off, and then, owing to the length of the line, we had to halt every ten or twenty yards.

We marched down the railway cutting for some distance and then turned off, across a country of which we knew nothing. Once, after crossing a ditch, we lost touch with those in front, but succeeded in joining up again. It was not until close on 2.0 that we reached our destination, although the distance cannot have been much more than three miles.

The officer in charge ordered us to hurry back as the dawn was breaking and we were close to the line. We started back in sections immediately we got rid of our burdens. By this time, a mist had gathered which made it very difficult to understand the lie of the land. So far as we could tell, we appeared to be on a low ridge, with the lines below us, but bullets were flying about freely and appeared to come from every direction. As we returned along the crest of the ridge, a furious fusillade broke out at the foot of the slope; rifles, machine-guns, shrapnel, and whizz-bangs all joined in, and the flashes and flares appeared on all sides.

There were half a dozen engineers' limbers and wagons on the road, and these stampeded at a breakneck pace, the drivers bent double, as low as possible, under the lee of their horses. We raced alongside, under the shelter of the wagons when we could manage it, but the road suddenly turned and narrowed, the wagons swerved to the side, and we had to leap on to the rough ground in order to avoid them. Down went one man on some wire, and another almost turned a somersault. I put my foot in a hole and wrenched it, falling to the ground. I could hardly walk, but two men seized me, one on each side, and I got along for a few yards. Then they managed to stop a wagon and hoisted me up.

Now there is no bottom to an engineers' wagon. One must sit either on a splash-board at each side or on the thin inch knife-board which forms the front. I sat on the latter, grasping the splash-boards with my arms outstretched and trying to cling to my rifle at the same time.

The drivers were in a proper panic and told me they had never been in that part of the world

I

before. Whenever possible we went at full gallop
and I was nearly bumped off, again and again.
Somehow, however, I managed to hold on, and
when we got nearer the town we slowed down.
The men on foot raced alongside for a mile or
more. After that they appeared to be scattered all
over the country, but they all got back in safety.
The worst of it was that we none of us had the
least idea where we, or the Huns, really were.

My friends set me down just inside the Menin
Gate and I managed to limp back to the cellars.
The next morning I had a slightly sprained tendon,
and I was on light duty for a day in consequence,
but I am more or less right again now.

I am now on guard in a miniature trench on the
top of the ramparts of Ypres. The wall in front
goes sheer down fifty feet or more into a moat, one
hundred yards broad. At my back the ramparts
slope upwards, dotted with big trees. Just above
me is one with an enormous label affixed to its
trunk.

Aesculus rubicundus
Marrioner rouge
Roode Kastenjiboom

The sun is shining and the birds are singing,
but beneath all other sounds there is one deep
undertone, the buzzing of innumerable flies.

On the other side of the moat there is a brickyard, some three hundred yards long. Broken
beams stick out of the piles of bricks at intervals,
but there is nothing else to show that the brickyard
was once a row of cottages. A dead cow lies half
in the water of the moat. Spurts of flame, every
now and then, disclose the position of a British
battery, and it is evident that some at least of the
desolation around has been caused by the efforts
of the Huns to locate the guns.

As I watch, a huge shell bursts in the moat,
raising a column of mud and water, and two others
find the brickfield amid clouds of red dust. Each
time a shell bursts, I duck while the debris patters
amongst the surrounding trees.

I suppose I am standing on the spot from which
generations of old-time burgher guards have
watched for raiding bands; but no medieval
raiders ever created the havoc of the modern
Huns. If I walk to the top of the Ramparts, pick-
ing my way amongst shell-holes—there is one
crater big enough to contain a house—I can look
over the town. Just below me is, or rather was,
the Church of St. Jacque. One pinnacle of the
tower is still left. The interior, seen from all
sides through the broken walls, is a pink heap
of brick and plaster. On one side is a small vestry.
The outer walls have gone, but I can see a

processional cross leaning against a corner of the inner wall, and in another stands the lamp which is carried before the Host.

In the city the roofs which remain are stripped of tiles. Not a house seems to remain undamaged, and through the broken walls of those least damaged one can see all the household goods. Everything seems to have been abandoned.

In the garden of a monastery hard by are the half-calcined remains of three beasts. The engineers have piled wood around and burnt them. In some cases houses have been fired intentionally, for the cellars are filled with the bodies of those who sought refuge, only to be caught by a shell, which shattered the dwelling above them, and shut them up alive, perhaps, in the tomb.

Above the town two towers still keep watch. Half of the one has gone, but two pinnacles are still intact. The other, that of the cathedral, still remains, a square mass, all its decoration gone, but its bulk untouched. For how long? Some fifty shells fell into the town last night, disturbing the rubbish and bringing down a few more walls. It is the strangest sight I have ever seen, but the worst thing about it is that buzzing undertone.

We go to the trenches at Hooge to-night. They tell us horrible details about them, but I don't suppose they are as bad as reported. No parcels have turned up. The transport brought up a few bags, but my section only got a parcel of books, so we shall have to subsist on Army rations for the next few days. I have seen no paper for a fortnight, and no one else has seen one of a date later than the 3rd.

We had quite a good concert in the cellars last night, and yesterday I had a swim in the moat, just before swimming was forbidden!

15*th June*, 1915.

I don't like this sector. It isn't at all healthy.
On the night of the 7th we crossed the moat by
a bridge of boats and followed a path which wound
amongst the ruins of some large school, down to
the railway cutting. We passed down the cutting
for some distance and then turned across country,
leaving Maple Copse on our right, and entered a
narrow belt of woodland which they say is Zouave
Wood.

Here we remained, lying in holes in the ground,
for two days. They were shallow holes, for the
most part, and in these we lived and slept. I had
one to myself, and it was more like a grave than
anything else, six feet long and eighteen inches
wide, only a foot deep, and with a cover of about
a foot at the head. As the grave was very wet,
I made up my mind to lie in the open, but after
poking about a bit I discovered a comparatively
good dugout unused, and with two others I moved
into this. It was all right so long as the weather
was dry, but we had two heavy thunder-storms,
and all the holes were flooded out. We dug a
sump-hole in one corner of our abode, and as

this filled baled it out, but it left us more than a bit muddy.

The Huns kicked up the dickens of a row sometimes. I was awakened by it on the second morning, and found that there was a regular firework display going on all around us. I soon realized that it was only a "s—— fight", and went to sleep again.

We got shots from all sides but one, and so far as I can tell, we were near the point of a small triangle, with the Huns on two sides of us. On the third night we moved into the point itself. The wood tapers out, and from the end we passed up the side of a water-logged communication trench into what appeared to be the neck of a bottle. Two trenches run out a short distance apart, but they do not actually join at the end. One stops near the stables at the Château of Hooge, and from that point there is a bit of communication trench to the stables themselves. We hold the stables, and the Huns own the Château, and they are only fifteen yards from the end of the trench. The stables are falling to pieces, but what is left of the Château is a big square fort of stone with sandbagged windows. The Huns are all around us, on five sides out of six, and bullets and trench-mortar shells can come from any of those five sides. We ourselves can fire

"The Wall", near Hooge, taken from Front Line in Sanctuary Wood, July 2nd, 1915

[To face page 136

at them, both in front and at the back, but luckily they dare not shell us, as they would probably get hurt themselves.

We had one man posted in the stable as a guard, and he was in full view of my traverse. Some joker amongst the Huns was amusing himself by firing at the top of the wall above his head, and while I watched he succeeded in dislodging half a dozen bricks, the pieces of which fell all about the guard. The latter could not move far without showing himself.

We only spent twenty-four hours in that trench, but that was quite enough. It rained hard, and I felt damp all day and was by no means sorry to leave. We were relieved at 1.0 a.m., and had a march of about nine miles to a field near Branthoec. On our way we had to pass through Zouave Wood, and the Huns were shelling, the shells bursting amongst the tree-tops and bringing some of the trees crashing down. The graves will not be healthy billets in future.

I had had no sleep for forty-eight hours, and reached the field more dead than alive. I just fell down on my wetter-sheet and slept until noon, but when I awoke I felt all right and perfectly ravenous. All our arrears of parcels had turned up, so we have more to eat than we know what to do with.

The only washing-place here is a pond in the next field, which is occupied by an Irish battalion. When I awoke the first thing I thought of was a wash and shave, but when I entered the Irish field I began to rub my eyes. There were some twenty big trees dotted about, and to every tree a man was tied up, by a rope twisted many times round his body and arms, so that his toes, in some cases, only just touched the ground. It was the first time I had seen No. 1 Field Punishment in operation, and the sight was not a pretty one.

We have been here four days, lying in the sun, washing and playing cards. Two attached A.S.C. men are running a Crown and Anchor Board. I very nearly broke their bank the other day; but they put on a limit, and that saved them. The Huns seem to have woke up and are putting over quantities of shells. Some of them nearly reach us here.

. Yesterday we were told we were "for it" on the 16th, and ever since then great preparations have been taking place. We have arranged to leave all our spare food and effects with a pal in the transport. Our section commander has been attached to the Salvage Corps, so he does not go up with us. He has appointed a substitute, and made a list of men who are to take charge of the section in turn, if things go wrong with those above them. I come some way down, so I am not likely to have much responsibility.

Everyone is suffering more or less from "wind up". It will be our first real show, and I suppose a certain amount of "wind" is natural. I certainly feel it myself, although I try not to show it. Anyway, we shall see what we shall see.

I have had an attack of "tummy", but am all right again now. Luckily I am generally fit, and fairly tough in most ways. It is blazing hot, but we do not move until evening, so that will not hurt us.

I am quite well, but don't feel so. On the 16th we supped full of horrors, and I feel almost competent to write another story of the descent into Hell.

We marched in the afternoon, four days ago, and halted in a field near the Dickebusche cross-roads for a meal. We each carried two days' rations, an extra belt of ammunition, and a couple of sandbags, so we were well loaded. The Huns were putting over quite a lot of promiscuous stuff, and a burst of shrapnel, during the halt, did in the adjutant.

We started again at dusk and passed down the railway cutting, but, instead of turning off into the fields, we went on as far as the Menin Road, at what is known as "Hell Fire Corner". A few hundred yards down the road we turned into the fields on the left, and found a resting place for the night in some shallow "jumping-off" trenches, a few yards back from the front line. It was very dark, and the trench was small, and sitting in a huddle I got cramp and felt miserable.

The Huns started by putting over big crumps

all around us. They seemed to aim for the relics of a building a hundred yards in the rear, and there the bricks were flying, but otherwise they did no damage. Still, they kept us guessing, and, knowing what was in front of us, I found sleep impossible.

Then at 2.50 a.m. our own guns started and kept up a heavy bombardment of the trenches in front until 4.15, by which time it was quite light. I don't know whether the Huns kept it up, too. In any case, one couldn't have heard them or their explosions: there was such a devil of a row going on.

At 4.15 a whistle blew. The men in the front line went over the top, and we scrambled out and took their places in the front trench. In front of us was a small field, with grass knee-high, split diagonally by an old footpath. On the other side of the field was a belt of trees, known as Y Wood, in which lay the first Hun trench.

In a few moments flags went up there, to show that it had been captured and that the troops were going on. Another whistle, and we ourselves scrambled over the parapet and sprinted across the field. Personally I was so overweighted that I could only amble, and I remember being intensely amused at the sight of a little chap in front of me who seemed in even worse case than myself.

Without thinking much about it, I took the diagonal path, as the line of least resistance, and most of my section did the same.

When I dropped into the Hun trench I found it a great place, only three feet wide, and at least eight deep, and beautifully made of white sand-bags, back and front. At that spot there was no sign of any damage by our shells, but a number of dead Huns lay in the bottom. There was a sniper's post just where I fell in, a comfortable little square hole, fitted with seats and shelves, bottles of beer, tinned meats, and a fine helmet hanging on a hook.

Our first duty was to change the wire, so, after annexing the helmet, I slipped off my pack, and, clambering out again, started to move the wire from what was now the rear, to the new front of the trench. It was rotten stuff, most of it loose coils, and the only knife-rests were not more than a couple of feet high. What there was movable of it, we got across without much difficulty, and we had just finished when we were ordered to move down the trench, as our diagonal advance had brought us too far to the right.

We moved down along the belt of woodland, which was only a few yards broad, to a spot where one of our companies was already hard at work digging a communication trench back to our old front line. Here there was really no trench at all. One or more of our own big shells had burst in the middle, filling it up for a distance of ten yards and practically destroying both parapet and parados. Some of us started building up the parapet with sandbags, and I saw the twins merrily at work hauling out dead Huns at least twice their own size.

There was a hedge along the back of the trench, so I scrambled through a hole in it, piled my pack, rifle, and other things, including the helmet, on the farther side, and started again on the wire. Hereabouts it was much better stuff, and it took us some time to get it across and pegged down. We had just got the last knife-rest across, when I saw a man who was placing sandbags on the parapet from the farther side swivel round, throw his legs into the trench, and collapse in a heap in the bottom. Several others were already lying there, and for the first time I realized that a regular hail of machine-gun bullets was sweeping over the trench.

I made a dive for my pack, but though I found that, my pet helmet had disappeared. Quite a string of wounded and masterless men had passed down the back of the hedge while I was working, and one of them must have thought it a good souvenir to take into hospital.

We all started work at a feverish pace, digging out the trench and building up some sort of shelter in front. One chap, a very nice kid, was bowled over almost at once with a bullet in the groin, and lay in the trench, kicking and shrieking, while we worked.

The attacking battalions had carried several more trenches and we were told that two at least had been held, but our own orders were to consolidate and hold on to the trench we were in at all costs. We could see very little in front. There was a wide field of long grass, stretching gently upward to a low mound of earth several hundred yards away. This was the next line. Away on the right front was Belleward Wood and Hooge Château, both above us, but the latter was partly hidden by the corner of Y Wood.

I had just filled a sandbag and placed it on the top of the parapet when I happened to glance down, and saw a slight movement in the earth between my feet. I stooped and scraped away the soil with my fingers and found what seemed like palpitating flesh. It proved to be a man's cheek, and a few minutes' work uncovered his head. I poured a little water down his throat, and two or three of us dug out the rest of him. He was undamaged except for his feet and ankles, which were a mass of pulp, and he recovered consciousness as we

K

worked. The first thing he said was in English:
" What Corps are you?" He was a big man, and
told us he was forty-five and had only been a soldier
for a fortnight.

We dragged him out and laid him under the
hedge. There was nothing else we could do for
him. He had another drink later, but he must
have died in the course of the day. I am afraid
we forgot all about him, but nothing could have
lived there until evening.

The Captain was the next to go. He insisted
on standing on the parados, directing operations,
and got a bullet in the lungs. He could walk,
and two men were detailed to take him down to
the dressing-station. One came back, to be killed
later in the day, but the other stopped a bullet
*en route*, and followed the Captain.

When we had got our big Hun out, he left a
big hole in the ground, and we found a dead arm
and hand projecting from the bottom. We dug
about, but did not seem to be able to find the body,
and when I seized the sleeve and pulled, the arm
came out of the ground by itself. We had to dig
deeper for our own sake, but there was nothing else
left, except messy earth, which seemed to have been
driven into the side of the trench. The man helping me turned sick, for it wasn't pretty work, but
I claimed a substitute, and between us we carted

out a barrowful in wetter sheets and dumped it under the hedge. After that I had had enough myself.

About 5.30 a.m. the Huns started shelling, and the new communication trench soon became a death-trap. A constant stream of wounded who had come down another trench from the north, passed along the rear. The Huns made a target of the two traverses (unluckily including our own), from which the communication trench opened, and numbers of the wounded were caught just behind us. The trench itself was soon choked with bodies, and it was easier and as safe to pass over the open above it.

The shelling got worse as the day wore on and several more of our men went down. They plastered us with crumps, shrapnel, and whizz-bangs. One of the latter took off a sandbag from the top of the parapet and landed it on my head. It nearly broke my neck and I felt ill for some time after.

It was grillingly hot and the air was full of dust, but although we were parched up, we dared not use much of our water. One never knew how long it must last. I came off better than most in that respect, for I had taken the precaution of carrying two water-bottles, knowing that one would never last me.

The worst of it was the inaction. Every minute several shells fell within a few yards and covered us with dust, and the smell of the explosives poisoned my mouth. All I could do was to crouch against the parapet and pant for breath, expecting every moment to be my last. And this went on for hours. I began to long for the shell which would put an end to everything, but in time my nerves became almost numbed, and I lay like a log until roused.

I think it must have been midday when something happened. An alarm was given and we manned the parapet, to see some scores of men retreating at a run from the trench in front. They ran right over us, men of half a dozen battalions, and many dropped on the way. As they passed, something was said of gas, but it appeared that nearly all the officers in the two front trenches had been killed or wounded, someone had raised an alarm of gas, and the men had panicked and run.

A lot of the runaways insisted on gathering by the hedge just behind us, in spite of our warnings not to do so, and I saw at least twenty hit by shrapnel within a few yards of us.

The Brigade-Major arrived, cursing, and called upon some of our own men to advance and reoccupy the trench in front. He led them himself, and they made a very fine dash across. I do not think more than twenty fell, and they reoccupied that trench and, I believe, the third also, before the Huns realized that they were empty.

In connection with this attack a rather amusing incident happened amongst ourselves. As soon as the man next me saw the attack commence, he yelled out: " They're our own men. Come on, we can't let them go alone." He was over the parapet in no time and dragged me half-way with him. As soon as the "gallant lad" was seen, he was ordered back, and the order was repeated by nearly all the men who were manning the parapet. He told me afterwards that it was the funniest of sights as he looked back, a dozen heads projecting over the sandbags, all with their mouths wide open, and all with one accord saying: " Come back, you silly ass!" He came back rather crestfallen.

The interlude was really a welcome one, and useful, too, for we realized then that nearly every rifle was clogged with dirt and entirely useless. We set to work cleaning at once, and this kept us occupied amidst the constant bursting of the shells. Our own guns were practically silent, and we supposed they were reserving ammunition, which was not too plentiful at the best of times.

Soon the runaways began to return. They had been turned back, in some cases, at the point of the revolver, but when their first panic had been

overcome, they came back quite willingly, although
they must have lost heavily in the process.   They
crowded into our trench, until there was hardly
room to move a limb.

It was scorchingly hot and no one could eat,
although I tried to do so.   All day long—the
longest day I ever spent—we were constantly
covered with debris from the shell-bursts.   Great
pieces fell all about us, and, packed like herrings,
we crowded in the bottom of the trench.   Hardly
anything could be done for the wounded.   If their
wounds were slight, they generally risked a dash
to the rear.   Every now and then we stood to in
expectation of a counter-attack, but none developed.

About 6.0 p.m. the worst moment of the day
came.   The Huns started to bombard us with a
shell which was quite new to us.   It sounded like
a gigantic fire-cracker, with two distinct explosions.
These shells came over just above the parapet, in
a flood, much more quickly than we could count
them.   After a quarter of an hour of this sort of
thing, there was a sudden crash in the trench and
ten feet of the parapet, just beyond me, was blown
away and everyone around blinded by the dust.
With my first glance I saw what looked like half
a dozen bodies, mingled with sandbags, and then
I smelt gas and realized that these were gas shells.
I had my respirator on in a hurry and most of our

own men were as quick. The others were slower
and suffered for it. One man was sick all over
the sandbags and another was coughing his heart
up. We pulled four men out of the debris
unharmed. One man was unconscious, and died
of gas later. Another was hopelessly smashed up
and must have got it full in the chest.

We all thought that this was the end and almost
hoped for it, but luckily the gas shells stopped, and
after a quarter of an hour we could take off our
respirators. I started in at once to build up the
parapet again, for we had been laid open to the
world in front, but the gas lingered about the hole
for hours, and I had to give up delving in the
bottom for a time. As it was it made me feel very
sick.

A counter-attack actually commenced as soon as
the bombardment ceased, and we had to stand to
again. My rifle had been broken in two pieces,
but there were plenty of spare ones lying about
now. I tried four, however, before I could get one
to act at all. All were jammed, and that one was
very stiff. As we leaned over the parapet, I saw
the body of a Hun lying twenty yards out in front.
It commenced to writhe and finally half-sat up. I
suppose the gas had caught him. The man standing next me—a corporal in a county battalion—
raised his rifle, and before I could stop him, sent

a bullet into the body.   It was a rotten thing to
see, but I suppose it was really a merciful end for
the poor chap, better than his own gas, at any rate.

The men in the front trenches had got it as
badly as we had, and if the counter-attack was
pressed, it did not seem humanly possible, in the
condition we were in, to offer a successful defence.
One man kept worrying us all by asking what we
were to do if the Huns did us in, whether surrender
or run!   Fortunately, our own guns started and
apparently caught the Huns massing.   The counter-
attack accordingly crumpled up.

In the midst of it all, someone realized that the
big gap in the parapet could not be manned, and
four of us, including myself, were ordered to lie
down behind what was left of the parados and cover
the gap with our rifles.   It was uncomfortable
work, as the gas fumes were still very niffy and
the place was a jumble of dead bodies.   We could
not stand up to clear them away, and in order to
get a place at all, I had to lie across the body of a
gigantic Hun.

As soon as things quietened down a bit, we had
a chance to look round.   Since the morning most
of the branches of the trees in the wood had gone
and many of the trunks had become mere splintered
poles.   Something else had changed also, and for
a time I could not make out what it was.   Then

it suddenly flashed across my mind that the thick hedge at the back of the trench had entirely disappeared. It was right in the path of the storm of gas shells and they had carried it away.

We managed to get some sort of parapet erected in the end. It was more or less bullet-proof, at any rate. At dusk some scores of men came back from the front line, wounded or gassed. They had to cross the open at a run or a shamble, but I did not see any hit. Then the Brigade-Major appeared, and cheered us by promising a relief that night. It still rained shells, although not so hard as before dusk, and we did not feel capable of standing much more of it.

As time wore on the shelling became more fitful, though it never actually ceased. It was comparatively cool again, and one could drink and even eat a little. My cap had gone in the general smash and I took another, which happened to fit.

No relief turned up, and about midnight two volunteers were asked for, to carry to the dressing-station a boy prisoner whose leg was smashed. There was considerable competition for the job, as we were told that the men selected could go on to the rear afterwards. A Fusilier and I were the lucky ones.

We managed to manufacture a sort of splint for the boy's leg and then tied his two legs together.

The Fusilier got him on his back and I took his legs.   It was a rotten job, as the poor wretch started screaming, and screamed until he fainted. After hoisting him out of the trench, we had to cart him across the open, which was a wilderness of shell-holes.   To make matters worse, I found I was as weak as a rabbit and could hardly carry myself.   Just as we left the trench, a long line of dark figures passed us.   They all wore the kilt, and we concluded that they were the expected relief.

We managed to get the boy as far as the old front-line, which was full of our own wounded, awaiting the doctor.   There we found a hospital orderly, and he suggested we should leave our burden with him.   We were thankful enough to do so, as the dressing-station was a full half-mile away.

After that my only thought was to get out of shell-fire as quickly as possible, and I made for the road by the way we had come the night before. The field was dotted with small parties of men who had just been relieved.   The ground was lower here and the stench of gas pervaded everything. Two small gas shells burst in the air above us, but I was too tired to worry about them.   The road when I reached it was full of troops, bonnets and caps, kilts and putties, some alone, some in twos and threes, some even in sections or small platoons.

These, however, soon lost whatever formation they had in the general rush. No one wanted to stay on the Menin Road longer than need be.

At one point a tree had fallen across the road and here there was a regular jam of men struggling past. Just then a shell burst close by, and someone shouted: "Gas!" We tried to pull on our respirators, but we were soon out of the immediate radius.

A Scot in front of me was hit by a flying piece of shell. "Gie us a hond, mate." Two of us took him by the arms and half-carried him until we reached the dressing-station at Hell Fire Corner. There was a hurried "Good-bye, Jock, good luck," and we dashed off again down the railway-line, stumbling over the sleepers as we went. Everything which added to the weight of the load was thrown away that night. Both road and line were strewn with clips of ammunition, tins of food, and articles of clothing.

The Hun shells seemed to follow us. One burst on the right of the line, the next on the left. The last one I saw that day burst one hundred yards away as we came out on the main road, south of Ypres. Hereabouts, some of the houses were still standing, and in one a light was shining. There was a rush for the door, and in the ruined kitchen we found a pump which still worked. The water

was of very doubtful quality, but no one had drunk
for hours, and its taste was sweet enough for
anyone.

When we left there it was quite light. Men
were lying about asleep all over the place. I saw
an officer asleep on a pile of sacks, just outside a
ruined house, and close by him three men lay in
a ditch. I struggled on by myself, and the farther
I went the clearer became the road. I passed a
dozen men of an Irish unit, who had stopped to
eat, and there was a small crowd at a wayside
watering-place. Single men of all sorts shambled
along, swaying from side to side, as if drunk or
half-asleep. A mounted transport man stopped
me and offered me a mount, but I couldn't have
mounted if I had tried, and if I could, I am sure
I should have fallen off at once.

At one place I passed some artillery dugouts.
The men were all outside. They stared, asked
questions, and gave me a tot of rum. The story
of the previous day had spread. I think we carried
it on our faces.

It took me five hours to reach the transport field.
Then I had a drink of hot tea, spread my wetter
sheet, and was asleep before I could take off my
boots.

I do not think many of us washed until the
evening. By that time I had recovered, more or

less, and after a wash and a shave a few of us went over to a neighbouring farmhouse and enjoyed an omelette.

We have lost half the battalion and nearly all our officers, including the Colonel and the Second-in-Command. Those of us who are left look worn and old, and our nerves are in tatters. We wake up with a start, and if a shell bursts a mile away we jump out of our skins. I am inclined to curse anything and anybody. I suppose that is nerves, too.

The next day we had the Brigadier round. We were all lying about, half-asleep, at the time, and with a consideration somewhat unusual in a Brass-Hat, he did not have us paraded. We were congratulated and patted on the back, and told that we had done very good work, and that next time we should have a chance on our own. What luck! He wound up by saying that troops that could stand that shelling could not be broken, and that he was afraid that we would have to go back into the trenches almost at once.

That sort of thing always reminds me of a story from home. Regimental Sergeant-Major, bullying wretched recruit: " Call yerself a soldier, do yer?" " No, sir, only a civilian, trying to do his bit." I do not excuse the priggishness of the reply, but the story does rather aptly represent the attitude of the

Regular towards us. They cannot understand that we are not soldiers and that we don't want to be soldiers, and though we shall carry on as well as we can, we don't like it, and are not in the least degree pleased at the prospect of a "brush with the Hun".

What we really like is the rest field after the "brush" is over. One can have no idea of the blessed peace of it, after a bad time. To lie on one's back in the sun, to watch the sunset, to wallow in the dirty washing-pool, to get a clean shave again, not to be tired all over, to feel against all expectation that one is still alive, to play a quiet game of poker again, or to try and do in the Crown and Anchor merchant!

On the 20th, after four days' rest, we marched up to the ramparts again. We were told that we were to remain there for the whole of that tour of duty, but if that were the order it was washed out again, for after a night in dugouts in the "Horseshoe", a bend of the ramparts, we marched up to Sanctuary Wood at Hooge, and spent the night in a sort of communication trench.

Going up I had a rather narrow shave. A bullet went clean through my pack from side to side, within half an inch of my back. It made about twenty holes in a folded wetter sheet. From the feel of it I thought it had actually cut my tunic.

The wood is a lovely spot, just behind the firing-line, but a sniper was taking liberties with us, and in many places it was unsafe to leave the shelter of the parapet. I fancy he shot from a tree on our right, but we could not spot him. All the shells from both sides seemed to pass over our heads, and not one fell in the wood itself.

Just behind us were two battalions of Regulars. They were very friendly, and I had two cups of tea with a party of them in a sort of "Maiden's

Bower" of leafy branches in the heart of the wood. We found we had been sent up for a special purpose. Another battalion, pals of ours, was to try and capture a small piece of trench, which had been won and lost again on the 16th. We were to support, and if the trench were taken, to relieve them and hold on. Everyone who had any knowledge of the lie of the land knew that the whole trench was enfiladed by the machine-guns at the Château, and although it might be possible to take it, it was impossible for any troops to remain there alive. They say that all sorts of protests against the futility of the attack were made, but some high Brass-Hat who, obviously, knew nothing of the ground, had insisted on it.

My hosts at tea told me that the attacking battalion had particularly requested that we might support them. It was a compliment which we might willingly have dispensed with, but we seem to have gained a reputation as "stickers", and this is one of its penalties. As a matter of fact, we get on very well with the Regulars. They are jolly good chaps. When we take over from another battalion of the division, we often find a message for us nailed up in the dugouts, with drawings of the badges of the two regiments above it.

The next night was far from pleasant, and now I know what it feels like to be part of a "forlorn

The Crater Trench, Hooge, September, 1915

[To face page 160

hope". We were in full kit at 8.0 o'clock, with an extra sling of ammunition, bombs, hand grenades, and empty sandbags. We heard the noise of the attack and what sounded like two counter-attacks, and waited on, in momentary expectation of the order to advance, until midnight, when we were told that we were not wanted, and held great but silent rejoicings. Later we heard that a platoon had attacked, but having lost most of its men in the first few yards, the remainder had retired, and the attempt had been abandoned.

Ever since the 16th I have been in command of the section as an acting N.C.O. It is some section now, I should think the poorest and weakest in the company. Still, the job relieves me of certain fatigues and gives me certain responsibilities, which are useful, as they occupy one's mind in unpleasant times.

The men are very quiet these days.

The following night, instead of being relieved ourselves, we were marched up to the bottle-neck at Hooge, and relieved one of our own companies there. This time we were on the other and worst side of the neck. The trench is so narrow that in most parts two men cannot pass each other and there is hardly any place to sit down. At one place it tunnels in darkness through some twenty yards of cellars, which are all that is left of the

L

houses of the village. There are no latrines, and all refuse has to be thrown over the parados, so the odours are both extensive and peculiar. The flies are legion, from great big flat bluebottle things, which blacken the sandbags with their bodies, to the smallest of midges, which look like dust or the mites in cheese.

Looking over the parapet one can see the water of Belleward Lake gleaming in the moonlight through the trees, but as an offset to this side of the picture several scarecrows are still hanging on the barbed wire. The Huns are only forty yards away and a good deal of bombing competition goes on, but in spite of their nearness, they appear to have shelled the trench on the 16th, when two shells landed right inside and wiped out a couple of traverses.

Apart from bombs, heat, and stench, we did not do so badly, for the Huns left us alone. We were relieved the following night and told we were to remain in the wood and do three days' fatigues. We were taken back to the communication trench where we had waited a few days before, and lay in the open. The fatigue was washed out, as it started raining, and rained incessantly all the next day. I rigged up my wetter sheet as a sort of roof in a corner of the traverse, and managed to keep a square yard of earth not more than damp, but to do that I had to bail industriously every two hours or so.

The next night someone discovered that there were some large empty dugouts only a few yards away, so we most of us moved into them, and, as things go, were fairly comfortable.

All sorts of rumours were afoot. One had it that the Division was to go out for a long rest on Sunday night. Another that we were all to have five days' leave, three men per company at a time. Another was that the Colonel and the Second-in-Command had both got decorations, and this at least proved to be true.

We went back to the ramparts the following night and found that we were to remain there instead of going out to rest. None of our parcels had come up, and we lived on rations which, for some reason or other, had been reduced to half the usual allowance. The ramparts themselves were by no means healthy. Early on the first morning the Huns threw in three hundred shells. One went through the wall of a house forty yards away, and most of the others were in the same neighbourhood. Usually they shelled for half an hour several times a day, and each time shelling commenced we had to dive into our dugouts, which were just under the lee of the ramparts. Unluckily, they were using gas shells a good deal, and several men have been caught in their dugouts by the fumes.

We occupied ourselves in building big dugouts, as we were uncomfortably crowded, and I succeeded in nearly breaking my nose. I had to dive from an unexpected shell a few yards away. It nearly deafened me, and in my haste I ran up against a big baulk of timber, which took most of the skin off and laid me out for the time being.

*6th July*, 1915.

The whole lot of us are in a pretty rotten condition and we are really not fit for anything. My inside seems to have gone wrong and I cannot eat. Nearly everyone is the same, so I suppose it is a sort of nervous exhaustion. We are all fed up with life, and particularly with the idea of having to spend our rest in such a spot. If the old Colonel had been with us still, it would not have happened, but we have a whole crowd of new officers just out from home in the place of those we lost, and they know nothing of the actual working conditions. Old D——, who was wounded at St. Eloi, has come back and has taken over the command of the section. I lose my job, but I am not sorry, as I shall have a pal in the section again.

We spent five days in the ramparts, under shell-fire most of the time, and with a dozen casualties. We were not supposed to move beyond the line of our dugouts and were often confined to the dugouts themselves. We have had crumps, gas shells, and the silent Austrian armour-piercing shells, which cannot be heard until they burst.

Every one of us has been occupied half the day in diving for his dugout; until now, if I hear a shell coming, my heart stops beating.

In spite of the prohibition, I managed to explore part of the town. One day I went to the Grand Place and along the road to the station. The Engineers have been very busy, and the main streets which were choked with fallen debris have been cleared to a great extent. The Grand Place, apart from its shell-holes, looks quite clean.

Some of the houses on the road to the station are hardly damaged. In many cases the owners have sent men into the town to collect their furniture, and on that side of the town the work is not so dangerous. On this side it is practically impossible.

I found one large house belonging to an iron-master, apparently, with two holes in the roof but with most of its furniture intact. The hall had been badly knocked about, and on the floor I picked up the stuffed head of a turtle, which had hung on the wall. I shall keep it as a souvenir. There was a huge amount of glass and china, but I suppose one of these next days a shell will finish it all.

There was an outhouse in the garden, which had been used as a wine cellar. The only entrance was a shell-hole, but I picked up a couple of bottles still

intact inside. I also found a set of rather pretty
gilt buttons in the ruins of what had been a drapery
establishment, but for the most part it was not
worth while salvaging anything that was not
capable of immediate use.

On the 1st July we went up to Sanctuary Wood
again, but this time to a different part. We spent
four days in a trench on the edge of the wood,
opposite a row of buildings which are known as
"the Wall", and are held by the Huns. They are
a good hundred and fifty yards away, and when
we took over we were told that it was a quiet bit
of the line. The shells flew over from all direc-
tions, but for the first two days we got nothing but
a few whizz-bangs. The trench itself bent in a
right-angle, and if not exactly comfortable was
much more so than the bottle-neck. I actually
managed to get a few hours' sleep in each twenty-
four.

Our numbers are so few that all four companies
had to be in the line at the same time, so there
was no possibility of a relief until our four days
were over. It was appallingly hot and our water
would not last out. There were one or two springs
or wells in the wood. They looked more like
stagnant pools than streams, and were not by any
means attractive, but we took to boiling the water
for tea. It was rather like yellow pea-soup, but

when boiled it cleared and formed a sort of scum on the top, which could be skimmed off. If the tea was made strong enough, there was no unpleasant taste, and it certainly did us no harm. Without it I do not know what I should have done.

The trench was so situated that there was no vestige of shade, and it was so hot that I lay in the bottom and gasped most of the day. Once I was forced to spare a quarter of an inch of water for an urgently needed shave, but water is too precious to use in that way, and I generally try vaseline instead.

In one way we did better. Our parcels were delivered and rations were increased. The programme one day was as follows: At 2.0 a.m., Stand to. I had some biscuits, cheese, and marmalade. From 3.0 to 6.0, Sleep. From 6.0 to 7.0, On guard. From 7.0 to 9.0, Tried to sleep, but the flies prevented. At 9.0, Breakfast, consisting of bloater paste, marmalade, and bread. From 9.30 to 2.0, Lay in the bottom of the trench, gasping. From 3.0 to 4.0, Read an old newspaper. At 4.0, A meal of tongue, cheese, bread and jam. At 8.0, Fatigue to Maple Copse for rations and water, a slightly risky job, but a relief from the monotony of things.

Our second two days were much more lively. A lot of shelling went on, and it came from such unexpected quarters that one never felt certain whether the shells were from our own or Hun guns. British shells were crossing our lines diagonally and falling on the Hun trenches in front. One or two Hun batteries in front were shelling our rear. Some 17-inch things were passing over bound for Ypres itself. Another battery was putting big crumps right across us to a small hill, three hundred yards on our left. Another on our right was pelting us with whizz-bangs, and another still farther to the right was sending small crumps right down the length of our trench, knocking branches off the trees above us and falling at first fifty yards beyond the right-angle, but later much nearer. These last came with a peculiar scream of their own, and always in salvoes of three. Every time we heard the scream we had to make a rush for the end of the traverse, which was the only shelter available.

As time went on the Huns improved their range, and the big stuff fell all around us, covering us with litter. Coming as they did, right down the trench, from one side, they were rather nerve-racking things. I don't know whether it was a result of the general state of my nerves, but I had the wind-up more properly than I ever remember before.

In fact, very little damage was done, except to

the trees.    One shell actually exploded on the parapet of the next traverse, but no one was injured. We were not sorry to be relieved, and this time we actually went back to the rest field.

Our march back was of the quietest, except for one incident.    The Menin Road was being shelled as usual, but we were travelling across country. We were approaching the railway-line, when suddenly there was a flash and a crash right on top of us.    I really thought a shrapnel had caught us, but no one seemed to be hit, and we realized that we were a few yards in front of one of our own batteries, which had fired over our heads.

That nine-mile march back is a bit of a strain. One man in the company has a tin whistle, and we try to sing, but for the last few miles it is difficult to keep awake, and one hasn't the energy left for anything else.

We are in rags.    Most of us have no seats to our trousers.    I picked up a pair of old cord breeches, so worn that they are open at the knees and have a six-inch gash down the side.    They are better than my trousers, which were in a positively indecent condition.    My tunic is literally falling to pieces.    I have sewn on the arms so often that the cloth will no longer hold together.    My shirt and vest are both thin, and as I have worn them night and day for a month, their condition is not pretty. Finally, my hair wants cutting. I must look a regular scarecrow.

The latest grievance is our leave. Very few of our men have had any so far, but most of the Regulars have had one leave at least. I spoke to one man to-day. He was just back, but had only come out in March. Every noncombatant who drives a motor-lorry seems to get leave every few months, but our own Division has had less than any other in the Army, and our own battalion less than any other in the Division.

*20th July*, 1915.

The day we got back, the scarecrows were inspected by the Divisional General. He cheered us all by promising us a three weeks' rest, with leave for all and a chance of leaving the "bloody triangle" for good. We got the usual buttering up, but we must have looked a strange lot of ragamuffins.

I managed to buy some salad the other day, a thing I had not been able to do for some time. The local villagers grow a lot of green stuff, but they will not sell, and as they all keep large families of tame rabbits, I suppose that is the reason.

We had a lot of wind and rain the first few days. I had one of those transparent oilskin capes which can be converted into a tiny tent, and when the weather was bad I used to lie up in that. One day, however, the wind was so strong that it was torn to ribbons, and I have to do without it.

One of my teeth fell out, so I got leave to see the Army dentist at Bailleul. A transport wagon was going with a crew of officers' servants, and I managed to get a seat in that. We reached there about 11.0, and as the dentist only gave me ten minutes, I had the rest of the day until 6.0 to myself. I indulged in a good lunch at the Hotel du Faucon, and made a number of purchases in the town. At the hotel were a lot of officers, who questioned me about the Hooge affair and congratulated us on our own show.

Coming back we brought a cargo of bottles for the officers' mess, and as the travelling was decidedly bumpy, I thought they would all be smashed. However, we got them all home safely, although the bottom of the wagon was strewn with trodden fruit and vegetables.

I received my first stripes as a Lance-Corporal (very much unpaid) that day. It should be one stripe only, but, as in the Guards, I believe, every Lance wears the two stripes of a full Corporal, with a little worsted grenade above them.

A large new draft has just come out, so our numbers are up again and I have met some old friends. I have succeeded in getting a new rigout. The tunic is rather like an Eton jacket, and the trousers are so tight that they catch me between the legs when I march, but they look much better than my old ones.

It appears that this rest was to be a period of intensive training, and after the first few days they started to work us pretty hard. Reveille at 6.0. Breakfast at 7.30. Parade at 8.30. Short route

Rest Field at Booseboom, near Dickebusche, September, 1915

Rest Field at Ouderdom, August 20th, 1915

[To face page 174

march or drill until 1.0, when we were dismissed
for the day. An N.C.O.s' class was formed, and
we drilled each other and, later, the men.

In the afternoons we generally managed some
amusement. One day I was taken to tea in
Renninghelst and introduced to Marguerite, a
pretty little girl who gives teas at Grandma's
cottage. Sometimes we organized an evening feed
at some farmhouse, and I generally managed a
game of cards during the day.

We have seen a lot of newspapers lately and a
large number of pictures, supposed to be connected
with the battalion, but in general they are pure
nonsense. One is a picture of a bull pup supposed
to accompany the men to the trenches. It never
did such a thing in its little life. It belongs to
the transport and lives in the transport field.

One is labelled : " Tommy must have his bath."
In fact, it represents a well-known character taking
a sunbath in the wood at Dickebusche, clad in
towels and an umbrella. Others called "The
——s doing something in the trenches" are
invariably pictures of the transport field or the rear.

In the same way most of the things that are said
about us in the papers are pure inventions. Each
one of us would think himself an ass if he told a
correspondent that he was "longing for a scrap with
the Huns", unless, indeed, he was pulling that

correspondent's leg, and talking "highfalutin", with that end in view.

Our latest occupation is sandbag filling. The Engineers are constantly engaged in fortifying farms and building redoubts all over these back areas, and each day some hundred of us are detailed to assist as builders' labourers. I have been out twice, starting at 8.30 and getting back at 4.0. One day I had a competition with the Company Sergeant-Major, who took off his coat to it for once. I filled fifty-six sandbags and loaded thirty of them into a limber, within a certain time. He beat me by a couple of bags. The next day I was so stiff that I could hardly use my arms at all.

Yesterday we were moved into a new field, not far from the old one. Old D—— and I joined forces. We got some hop poles and old P.O. bags, and with the aid of our wetter sheets, constructed a strong and quite comfortable bivvy or shelter. Its construction entailed a lot of work and we regarded it with great satisfaction, particularly having regard to the fact that it has rained every day for a week or more.

There is a farm adjoining the field which is specially reserved for our own use, where we can buy bread, beer, stout, and coffee, and at least a dozen women bring round eggs, oranges, chocolate, and bread.

To-day the news comes that our rest is washed out. We are needed in the line and go back to-morrow night. So all the labour expended on our new camp appears to have been wasted. The one bright spot seems to be that we are not going right into the Salient this time, but farther south, close to St. Eloi. Whatever happens there, we shall only get shells from one direction, and need not fear a shot in the back. I don't care much about anything else now.

The usual number of latrine rumours are current. (1) That the rate of leave is to be increased. (2) That the whole brigade is to go home in six weeks. (3) That we are merely going in for a short and cushy time, whilst others make an attack elsewhere. (4) That Kitchener's Army is to make a big attack somewhere. Nowadays one never believes any story, however likely it may sound.

*3rd August*, 1915.

On the 21st July we marched south and bivouacked in Scottish Wood, in front of Dicke-busche and quite close to Elzenwalle Château. We relieved the Queen Victoria Rifles, who told us that things in front were fairly quiet, but that the Huns occasionally used "sausages". Their description of these and their effects was not altogether pleasing.

There were some good dugouts in the wood, and we were quite comfortable there for three days. I was on fatigue one night, and although a Lance-Corporal I had to carry sandbags. We were ordered to find twenty-seven men more than our total strength, so we had to include in the party a number of junior N.C.O.'s. Sandbags sound an easy burden, but the ordinary load is fifty, and the seventy-five which we each carried are a pretty heavy burden. When we dropped them at the back of "Q3", near the old Bus, I had had quite enough for the evening.

The weather was rotten, and our roof started to leak one night and gave us all a showerbath. We managed to cure the worst of it the next day.

After three days in the wood, we did three more in the front line, and there the weather was better. The first day, the Huns sent over a few whizz-bangs, and one of these took off the sandbags from the parapet of the next traverse, but after the "bloody triangle" the place appeared a haven of rest.

We saw a Hun plane brought down. It caught fire and turned turtle, but was still apparently more or less under control. The smells were much better about there, but the flies were terrible. In one hour I squashed some thousands on the sandbags, but the carnage appeared merely to attract, and the bodies of the dead were soon hidden by thousands of the living. Because of them, I only got one hour's sleep the first day, but I managed three and a half hours the next, and I know by experience that if I can get three or four hours of sleep in the twenty-four I can carry on all right.

The grass had grown so high between the lines that one could only just see the Hun parapet by the aid of a periscope, and then only in little patches. It was rather a nuisance, as one always suspected the presence of a Hun patrol, but it must have been equally bad for them.

Our second day in the line was an exciting one. They had shelled the trenches all around us, inter-mittently, all the morning, but had left us severely alone. A battalion of the Northumberlands, who were in our old trenches next door, had been rather busy with their rifles the night before, and in the early morning (as we found later) they had put up a sheet facing the Hun lines inscribed with the words: " Got strafe the Kaiser." They received their reward late in the afternoon, and as the centre of the disturbance was only a couple of hundred yards away, we were not exactly pleased.

The Huns started about 5.30 p.m. with big crumps, and later added shrapnel, small shell, whizz-bangs, and sausages. The last are shells from a Minenwerfer, and are horrid things. One hears a gentle ping, for they are fired by compressed air, I believe. Then a couple of hundred feet in the air one sees a black thing which looks like a German sausage. It travels very slowly, turning over and over, and then falls almost perpendicularly. When it explodes it makes as much noise and more vibration than a big crump. It forms an enormous crater, burying everyone in the neighbourhood, and scattering razor-like pieces of steel all over the place.

They must have sent over more than forty of these things in about an hour and a half, and we thought the adjoining trenches must have been knocked to pieces. We had a special guard out, for one can tell approximately where a sausage will fall, and if one has warning, there is plenty of time to move down the trench, out of its immediate radius. One could hear the shouts from the next trench: " There she comes." " Look out," and then a bewildering crash.

About dusk the wounded started coming out along the back of our own trench, and we heard that they had suffered rather heavily, a lot of men having been buried by the explosions.

We were all feeling a trifle exhausted at night, and about 10.0 o'clock I was lying in my dugout with another man when there was a big explosion, and the whole ground rocked as if with an earthquake. We tumbled out, seized our rifles, and manned the parapet. A huge cloud of smoke was rising to the stars from a small advanced trench on our left front. We realized at once that the Huns had sprung a mine, but star-shells were coming out of the smoke, and the rifles were hard at it, so we knew the trench had not been wiped out. We stood to, waiting for an attack, but our own guns broke out almost at once and no attack was attempted. Apparently the mine exploded just in front of the parapet, and only a few men were hurt.

Our third day was fairly quiet and we suffered chiefly from our own guns. There was a battery somewhere in the rear—they said it was a Belgian one—which would persist in firing short. Several of its shells burst behind us. One, a shrapnel, burst right over our heads, and when they reached the Hun trenches, the explosion was a pitiful sort of pip-squeak, which did not seem capable of doing any damage. Another thing we suffered from was ricochets. One shell from the Huns struck the ground in front and bounded right over the trench. We were on the slope of the hill and I saw several strike the ground behind us several times before exploding.

My next three days were a new experience. I was detailed as Corporal of a small guard of four men, which was stationed at an Army watering-place, on the main road north of Dickebusche. We had instructions to prevent tampering with the pipes, to supply water to the Army carts, and to see that it was properly chlorinated before delivery. One man was on guard for two hours at a stretch, but there was very little to do, and as Corporal I did not even take my turn at that.

The Guard Room, where we lived, was at a little house close by, kept by an old man and his son. We could buy eggs, vegetables, and lots of canned goods next door, and Bass of a sort could be pro-cured three doors away. One dinner consisted of steak, obtained from some gunners, whose battery position was near-by, kidney beans and new

potatoes. I hadn't tasted the like since I left
England.

The only drawback was Hun "frightfulness",
which seems to have increased of late, and the
terrific gunning almost next door, which kept us
awake at night. Rumours of the wildest description poured in from passers-by. We heard stories
of an attack with liquid fire, somewhere near
Hooge, with burnt corpses and whole battalions
destroyed. It was not until some days later that
we heard the true story of the first liquid fire attack,
and we were quite satisfied to remain where we
were as long as they would allow us.

After a couple of days of this sort of holiday,
however, we went back to the trenches, this time
in the support line where, for a further three days,
we had a fairly lively time, but luckily without
casualties. Shells from both sides flew over our
heads, apparently only a few feet above them, and
mines exploded at odd moments throughout each
day. The Huns were using armour-piercing shells
in an endeavour, we were told, to find our saps,
and springing mines prematurely for the same
purpose.

Every time a mine exploded we had to stand
to, but although each explosion was followed by a
burst of rifle-fire, nothing further ever happened.
They worried us, too, with sausages, and although

none fell near enough to do any damage, the *morale* of the troops was not improved by having to dodge round the traverses in an effort to avoid them.

We were relieved by a North Country battalion of Kitchener's New Army—the first I have seen. They were rather quaint birds. They talked as if the War would be over in no time, now that they were out, but as soon as they got into the trench, a lot of them jumped on the fire-step and started firing at our own line, just in front. We had to pull some of them down.

On relief, we marched to a field near Vlamer-tinghe, some five miles to the rear. It pelted with rain and there was no shelter, so I strung two wetter sheets together and crawled in between, with my head protruding from the top. It was rather damp and uncomfortable, but I managed to get some sleep. Before daybreak I found that the water was getting into my nest, so I got up and wandered into an adjacent farmhouse, where I found a red-hot stove and a number of men drinking coffee.

After breakfast a consignment of parcels was delivered, and this included one for me. I found that it came from a girls' school, where some young friends of mine were pupils. It was really a wonderful parcel. Each girl seemed to have con-tributed something—chocolate, sweets, biscuits, tobacco, cigarettes, socks, cakes, and soap, particu-

larly soap. I had some difficulty in distributing
the last, but what we could not carry ourselves we
handed over to some Regulars in the next field.

It rained all day, but in the afternoon we moved
on, skirting the north of Ypres, and took up our
residence in some crazy dugouts on the bank of the
Yser Canal, which we crossed by a pontoon bridge.
The dugouts were not even splinter-proof, mere
shelters from the sun, and along the top of the bank
there ran a trench, into which we were ordered
for shelter whenever shelling started. There must
have been a dozen batteries within a comparatively
short distance, and the Huns had a nasty habit of
putting over big shells in the middle of each afternoon in an effort to locate them.

There is plenty of water in the canal, although
it is more or less stagnant. It breeds clouds of
mosquitoes, which bite like fun, and though it is
nice to be able to get a wash when one likes, there
are too many floating carcasses of various sorts.
The men discovered a dilapidated punt, and went
paddling about in it, using planks for paddles. I
saw it right in the middle, when a small Hun shell
plunked into the water twenty yards away. That
amusement was then vetoed, but a certain amount
of bathing takes place every day.

Except for night fatigues and aeroplane guards
there is nothing much to do. I walked over to

Brielen the first day, and found still open a number of shops where one could buy vegetables and other things. The next day a shell caught the place, and both the vegetables and the little girl who sold them were scattered to the winds. Most of the day we spent playing bridge, with some profit to myself, and taking it all round it was a very cushy time. I have just been put in command of another section and march with them to-night.

I have been having a regular summer holiday.
The battalion left the Canal and went into reserve
trenches, north of the Salient, but I did not. Two
sections, including my new one and the R.S.M.,
marched only a mile and took over a little trench
in a bit of woodland near an abandoned farm called
Frascate Farm. There is supposed to be a reserve
ammunition dump in the neighbourhood, but it
is not obtrusive, and unless it is kept in the farm
I really don't know where it is. We were the
ammunition guard. There was a dugout in the
trench for each two men, and a few over, and they
were not common ones, either, the roofs and sides
being of wood, properly carpentered. Twenty
yards away on the other side of our strip of woodland was a parallel trench much deeper, for shelter
during shelling, but commonly used for cooking
purposes.

My new section is a good one and is composed
of very nice chaps. I had to report at H.Q. one
day, walking up by communication trench, and the
Adjutant informed me that the two sections had
been selected, because they were composed of men

who had been out a long time and deserved a rest. We certainly got one, and it was the pleasantest time I had spent since we came out. So far as shelling is concerned, the Huns plastered the surrounding country, but we ourselves never got anything but an occasional burst of shrapnel, and none of that within a hundred yards.

For the most part the weather was good, fine and plenty of sun, and the only drawback to a period of perfect peace was the flies. There were a lot of mosquitoes, but thousands of flies, tiny little ones like dust. They didn't bite, but they crawled over a newly-shaven face and irritated badly. On one occasion I was beaten altogether and fled to my dugout, where only common flies and mosquitoes congregate.

We were in full view of Ypres about a mile away, and what is left of its towers. On the 12th we watched a bombardment by the big seventeen-inch gun, which lasted most of the day. One could see the shells as they fell. By the end of the day the relics of the Cloth Hall had considerably decreased in size. In the early morning we could see the tower of the Cathedral and the whole of one side, pierced with windows. In the afternoon there did not seem to be anything left but the tower. Their shooting was quite good. I saw two shells which appeared to go clean through the tower.

The Apex Trench, Sanctuary Wood, Hooge, September, 1915

[To face page 190

One hit the top corner and seemed to rebound towards the Cloth Hall next door. A big block of masonry slipped down, but it did not alter the appearance of the tower itself, which speaks something for the solidity of its construction.

Huge fragments of the shells flew all over the place, and one fell within three hundred yards of us, after making a noise in the air like the passage of a train.

Most of the day we slept or played cards. We introduced the R.S.M. to the game of *vingt-et-un* which, like the heathen Chinee, he did not understand. The result was rather disastrous to both sections, most of whom were anxious for the next pay day.

Each section was on duty on alternate nights. Generally speaking, it was merely a question of reporting at the ration dump at La Brique and forming a carrying party from thence to the trenches, but on several occasions we were out until two in the morning trench digging. I went up once with a party and dug a new trench in front of the firing-line. Thereabouts the lines are some three hundred yards apart and are separated by a sort of swamp. I fancy the Huns must have been out on the same game, as no shots were flying.

We were told that the General had been round and stated that he had a surprise for us when we left there, but nowadays we don't expect much fruition from any promises of that sort.

Another night we dug a connecting trench at an angle in the line. Things were rather lively, the Huns indulging in fierce bursts of rifle-fire, and every now and then we had to hop into such shelter as we could find and stand to. Their lights were rather brilliant. They must have some sort of captive balloon or kite and send up chains of coloured lights by a cable. I suppose it was some sort of signalling device. Then they had star-shells of green, red, and white and about five searchlights close together.

On our last night things became very lively. It was my night at the ration dump and I found everyone with the wind well up. They were shelling Ypres fiercely, and all the roads, and a furious row was going on in the direction of Hooge, where the horizon was a blaze of light. They said that an attack was in progress over there.

Our chief difficulty at Frascate Farm was for supplies. We could not get any clean clothes, we were reduced to half-rations in some things, and very few parcels came up. As for linen, my towel had had a month's use and I hadn't had a clean handkerchief for a fortnight.

Much to our regret they relieved us on the 19th and we marched to a new rest field near Ouderdom.

As a bivouac it is an improvement on the last, but it has rained in torrents and is rather damp. We have slept in the open ever since March, and it will seem strange to sleep under a roof again.

There is a comfortable inn in the village, where the beer is better than most in Flanders, but the peasants are sullen and Hun-like as usual. We have heard nothing more of the "surprise", but all leave is stopped, and that does not look promising.

A rather curious thing happened yesterday. We saw a little toy balloon falling over this field. It reached the ground in the adjoining field, the bivouac of another battalion. Some of the men made a dash for it, but were called off by an officer. "Don't you know better than to meddle with mysteries like that?" As soon as it reached the ground a puff of wind caught it and it rose and sailed off towards the south.

I am Company Orderly Corporal for this week and have my hands pretty full. I have to do the donkey work for the Orderly Sergeant, give out orders, collect passes, detail fatigues, make lists of things wanted, collect the sick for the M.O.'s parade, etc., etc. However, most of my week will be passed in the trenches, as we go up to-morrow, and there the O.S. and the O.C. cease from troubling.

We have been back in the old spot at the tip of the Salient, but the whole district has changed its appearance since we were there last. We held a trench along the front of Zouave Wood. On our left the front line was represented by the old communication trench to Hooge. On our right was Sanctuary Wood, and there the trenches were in advance of ours, although our old trench in front of the Wall had been abandoned. All the old front trenches appear to have been rendered untenable, so there is a wide space between the two forces, and at night patrols roam about between the lines, and occasionally a fierce little bombing fight develops between them. No Man's Land is honeycombed with unoccupied trenches, and the slope of the hill up to Hooge looks like a ploughed field. It is churned up by shells and covered by the debris of a big mine.

Right in the middle of No Man's Land, in a disused trench, we had a listening and bombing post. I did twenty-four hours there in charge of a party of six. We had our rifles and several bags of bombs, but none of my men was a bomber, and I doubt if we could have used the bombs very effectively.

It was a really ghastly spot, particularly in the moonlight. On two sides of us, but some distance away, were the woods, or what had been woods. One is now a forest of masts, without branches or leaves, and many of them broken in half and blackened by fire. All around us were abandoned trenches—many of them filled with the dead— underground passages, and shell-craters. Close beside us was a crater fifteen feet deep, with a pool of water at the bottom, and scattered about in the water and around I saw a box of bombs, spades, a shovel, broken rifles, and a human head without a body.

Just to our rear, about four yards away, was a row of graves, Hun-made apparently, for they were mere mounds of earth, and, from one, another head protruded.

Throughout the night hundreds of rats scuffled about, and at intervals we heard the sounds of patrols and burial parties. Half the night, against the skyline on the ridge, we could see the burial parties at work, cast into sharp relief by the light of the star-shells. We could hear the noise made by the Hun transport quite plainly, and from the sounds I should think they were working in their trenches. I could hear voices and a good deal of banging and hammering.

There were two other posts, some distance from ours, but these were not used in the daytime at all. We were practically isolated, and after going in at night, could not move for twenty-four hours. The daytime was most unpleasant. The heat was terrific and there was absolutely no shelter. We had nothing to do but to lie still as low as possible, in order to evade observation by the planes, which hovered over us all day long.

There was any amount of shelling, chiefly from our own side, and I think we must have got hold of some new explosive, unless our shells are of much better quality than they used to be. The results are much greater, and the explosions pro-duce a curious yellow smoke and seem to shake the earth for miles around.

One gun was firing very short and the shrapnel exploded right over our heads. Another shell hit the ground behind us and jumped our trench before exploding in front. We were not sorry to be relieved, but for the most part the day was merely very wearisome. On getting back, however, we escaped guard and could sleep instead.

The weather was wonderful. There was no rain, and I read my letters by moonlight when they came up with the rations. The wood at our back was full of blackberries, just about ripe, and some of us went out at night and gathered them by the light of the moon.

The battalion on our left had a rather bad time. The Huns shelled the old communication trench every day and the men holding it were changed each night, after suffering heavy casualties. They left our own bit of trench alone, and while we remained there we played quite a lot of quiet poker.

We were told that we were to remain in as a battalion for an indefinite period, but one company at a time was to go out for a three days' rest, so after six days in Zouave Wood we marched out to a field near the Dickebusche Road, getting there at about three in the morning.

It had turned wet and the roads were very heavy, so we stumbled along most of the way, and I was more tired than I have been for some time. Once I came a cropper, headlong in the mud, and must have jerked out the magazine of my rifle.

It appears that our great "surprise" was promised to other units of the brigade also, but it has come to nothing. We are to go in again, for twelve days this time, but of course that rumour, like so many others, may be quite baseless.

In this field each section is allotted a large tarpaulin called a "bivvy sheet", and some scaffold poles, and ordered to set up a tabernacle for itself.

It would be quite comfortable, but our sheet leaks in sundry places, and as it has usually rained, there is a constant shower spray within. Still, we don't have so bad a time.

Yesterday I got up at 8.0 and went and had a comfortable breakfast of bread and milk and fried eggs at the little shop which we used when on water guard some time ago. There is a restaurant called the "White House" at the end of Dicke-busche Lake, which is kept by a refugee from Brussels. There are rumours about him, but he can cook all right, and I had a most excellent lunch there one day.

Last night I had an invitation to celebrate a birthday at the water-guard shop, and we spent a most festive evening with wine and song.

To-day we go in again. I have had my morning wash and "straf", the water coming from a pond the colour of pea-soup. I have drawn a new sort of smoke-helmet, with glass eye-pieces and an indiarubber breathing-tube, cigarettes, matches, and rifle-rag for my section. I have attended a parade for smoke-helmet instruction and practice.

Leave is open again, but at the present rate of progress it will be some months before I get away. The men just back from leave tell me that the Junction was crowded with men going home, but that nine out of ten of them were of the A.S.C.

or the R.A.M.C., men who are seldom or never under fire, live at the rear, and go home regularly every three months. The papers rave about the R.A.M.C., but they do not understand that in ordinary trench warfare these men seldom come nearer to the firing-line than the ration dump, and that the stretcher work is done by the battalion stretcher-bearers, who are ordinary infantrymen. This, of course, does not apply to the battalion M.O., who is in or near the line with the battalion. Even the job of battalion stretcher-bearer is regarded as a soft job for the work-shy, although in an attack it is dangerous enough.

Our guns have been strafing the Huns unmercifully of late, and the latter retaliate with a small hurricane of shells, but that sort of thing does not seem to get us much forrarder with the War.

*10th September*, 1915.

We have had about enough for the present. We were in trouble almost as soon as we left the rest field, and we have had our fill of it ever since. To start with, ten minutes after we left the field a big shrapnel burst close by. A short distance farther on we found that the Huns were shelling the roads. At Kruistrat, where we turned off towards Bridge 14, over the old canal, we had to halt for a long time in a mixed crowd of troops and transport, who were held up by the shelling.

When we did start again, we moved in parties, two sections at a time, right through the shelled area. One shell nearly caught us, bursting only a few yards away. It was rather windy work in the dark. It had rained most of the day and the night was black as pitch, and we were slipping and falling all over the place. I fell flat down twice. Once we saw half a mile of the horizon, flooded with a brilliant orange light for several seconds, but no one seemed to know its cause. It may have been an incendiary shell, but if so, I don't know why they should use it, as there are no buildings left at the tip of the salient.

Then we lost our way in the darkness and had to retrace our steps for some distance. It began to rain in torrents, and by the time we got in we were soaked to the skin and our boots squelched at every step.

We were placed in a support trench in Sanctuary Wood, and I found what looked like a good dugout, but after a couple of hours, the roof started to drip all over, and in the morning I found that I was lying in a pool of water half an inch deep.

The rain continued all the next day and the dugout was useless. Towards evening it ceased, but it was impossible to get dry again. I had one dry pair of socks, and these I drew on over another pair, after wringing the latter out, but although the result was more comfortable than the squelching, it was not much of a remedy for the wet. I tried to dry my others in the open, but by night they were as wet as ever. The only real comfort we got was an occasional tot of rum.

Our guns had given the Huns "hell" all day, and that afternoon they retaliated with a flood of shells much worse than our own. They burst in the tree-tops, smashing the branches and breaking off the trunks all around us. It is not at all a nice sensation to be shelled in a wood, with all the bursts overhead.

That night—the third—we were moved up a

Signallers' Dugout, Sanctuary Wood, Hooge, September, 1915

[To face page 202

waterlogged communication trench into a front-line trench, called the "Apex", which jutted out towards the Hun lines and from which we could fire both back and front. The trench itself was a sort of deep gully, and the traverses opened out of and above it on one side only. I had three men with me in my own traverse, but the adjoining one had been completely wrecked by a shell and was empty, so that the rest of my section was entirely isolated from me.

At about 10.0 p.m., after seeing my men safely in, I went to my dugout in the main trench to get some food. I had just begun to eat, when suddenly without any warning the Huns started to send over a storm of whizz-bangs and shrapnel, which seemed just to clear the parapet. I crawled back into the traverse on my hands and knees and seized my rifle. They kept it up for a quarter of an hour, while we crouched in the bottom. Then we thought we heard a cheer and manned the parapet at once. We could not see more than a few yards into the undergrowth in front of us, and, expecting an attack, started quick fire into the blackness of the night. The Platoon Sergeant arrived with extra slings of ammunition, and I should think we must have fired fifty rounds each. My rifle never jammed, which was surprising, considering the weather conditions. It was rather exciting, as no one dreamed but that an attack was intended. If it was, it never developed. We were all above the parapet, and every now and then someone thought he saw something moving in front; but one can fancy anything at such a time. In half an hour everything was quiet and no damage had been done, to us, at any rate.

We stood to most of the night and a regular tropical downpour commenced. The clouds seemed almost on the ground, below the tree-tops, and when one passed over, it was like a huge shower-bath. We were soon wet through again, but as we had never been dry since our arrival in the wood, it did not make much difference.

When the dawn appeared, we were very pleased to see it, but it did not do us much good. The rain stopped for a time, but the trenches were half-full of water, and often it reached to the knees.

About 5.0 our guns started their morning strafe. The first shell fell just in front of our own parapet, the second—a huge lyddite—fifty yards to our own rear. We were ordered to move down the trench, and luckily for us we did so in a hurry. The next shell fell in the trench itself, and as we paddled down the communication trench, the Hun guns joined in and got our range beautifully.

An hour or so later, when we returned, I found that three small shells had burst right inside my traverse. The place was in a shocking mess, and a rifle which had somehow got left behind had been broken into a dozen pieces. One poor wretch was caught by a piece of our own shell before he could get away.

Three times that day we had to evacuate the trench during a bombardment, and we seemed to spend most of our time wading in the floods. By evening a considerable part of the wood must have disappeared, and quite half of the trees were lopped of their branches and tops.

At night we were relieved and ordered back to the support trench, but just before we moved I was sent in charge of a party to the listening post for a few hours until the proper relief arrived from the rest field. By this time the flesh of our feet had become so sodden with the wet that it was very painful for some of us to walk at all. To get to our post we had to wade through a foot of mud, and when we got there we found that the old trench was full of water. All we could do was to sit in the mud, with our feet in the water, for three solid hours, until we were relieved about twelve.

I had had practically no sleep for three days and nights and could only keep myself awake, in spite of the discomfort, by moving my arms constantly. I suppose that if I had fallen asleep, I should have fallen into the trench, and, like as not, have been drowned or asphyxiated, for none of my party were in any better case than myself.

When we got back to the support trench, I took off my boots and two pairs of stockings, coated my feet with vaseline, pulled on another pair of wet socks, thrust my feet into a sandbag, pulled another over that, and was soon as warm as toast. I slept like a top, and by morning the socks and I myself were both dry. It was not pleasant putting them into wet boots again, but luckily the day was fine and hot, and I got really dry for the first time since we left the field.

After that we spent three more days in a front trench, but apart from a few bursts of whizz-bang fire, we had a much more quiet time and lay about in the sun most of the daytime, although the continuous bombardment went on all around us.

Last night we were relieved and returned to the Dickebusche field, which is now somewhat congested, as the whole battalion is out. I have lost my extra wetter sheet. It was torn to ribbons in that traverse. Luckily my pack was in the dugout underneath and escaped.

I find myself a full corporal, this time with pay.
When we came out, I think I was more done
up than I ever remember to have been before, and
even now I feel rather as if I had been used up and
thrown away. There is nothing really the matter
with me, except a touch of rheumatism in the
arm, but I fancy the whole lot of us feel much
the same. Two sergeants nearly collapsed before
we left the line and were sent on in advance. They
did not reach the field until forty-eight hours later.

There has been something of a row with the
Brass-Hats. It appears that when we were in we
were ordered to dig a communication trench along
part of the front of Zouave Wood, but, for some
reason or other, the digging was omitted. As a
result, instead of returning to the transport field, we
were ordered to remain where we were and go up
*en masse* every night until the trench was finished.
That means some six miles out and six miles back
with some four hours' digging in between, and in
our then condition the task did not appeal to us at
all. Somehow we managed it, and after three days
we were allowed to return to the transport field,

although a digging party still went up every night.

It was rotten work. There had been an old trench which had been knocked to pieces, and the earth was full of old sandbags, partly decomposed bodies, and stringy things, which made digging difficult or almost impossible. In places the stench was appalling, and it was constantly necessary to cut through the roots of trees and undergrowth in order to make progress possible. We did a great part of the work and then it was taken over by some other unit.

The weather has been much better. Every day we do a route march, though not a very long one, and half the day seems to be taken up with inspections and parades, as if the Powers intended us to be "for it" shortly. We still find time for an occasional game of cards and a meal in a local *estaminet* or farmhouse. I had one at Branthoec last night.

The continuous bombardment still goes on, but although the Huns put over a good many shells into the back areas, they have not touched us here so far.

*25th September*, 1915.

We are all, metaphorically speaking, shaking
hands with ourselves in the satisfaction of being
still alive. We have taken no part in the actual
attack to-day and are now in reserve, but for the
last six days we have been holding what are
probably the worst trenches in the worst part of the
whole British front, under a "continuous bombardment". I suppose the idea of the thing is all right,
but it involves a pretty heavy cost, as the Huns'
retaliation is as continuous as our attack.

For us it has meant six days of continual strain,
six days practically without sleep, six days without
a wash and with no drink except chlorinated water,
six days and nights with our boots on, crouching
at the bottom of a trench, unable to do anything
and with the full knowledge that the next moment
was likely to be our last.

The General is reported to have said some time
ago that those trenches could not be held for more
than two days in ordinary times without a relief,
but we have had to stick it for six days under
extraordinary conditions. Several men went down
with nervous breakdown, and I am surprised that

many more did not follow them. Still, the luck of the battalion has held. Our casualties were only about one hundred, or one in four, and the proportion of killed was small.

The first night we found ourselves in a trench opposite Bellewarde Lake. The next company held the big Hooge Crater, and the others were in support behind. The ground all round was in a horrible condition, a mere waste of overlapping craters, churned and flung up in small hillocks, overlooking evil-smelling water-holes. It was strewn with bones, broken tools, burst sandbags, and pieces of torn clothing. At one place in the trench someone had started to dig a recess for a latrine, but had stopped abruptly, and from the end of the cutting there hung down a discoloured trouser leg, with a shank of bone still inside it and a rifle with a broken and clotted bayonet attached.

The ground was strewn with corpses, and at night we went out and buried some of the nearest. One we found was garbed in the costume of a Sister of the French Red Cross, but how she came there it is difficult to understand, unless she had been buried a year ago and disinterred by an explosion.

The bombardment went on all day and all night, with bursts of extraordinary energy about four or five times a day. Our shrapnel burst generally almost above our heads, and with each explosion one could feel a blast of hot air fan one's cheek. When our guns were most energetic we were ordered to take refuge in a narrow communication trench, and there we sat or squatted for hours at a time, with nothing to see but a bit of blue sky above us and the Hun shells crashing all around. The big crater was one of the worst spots, I believe, although I was not in it myself. Four officers were killed there in one dugout by a single shell which made a direct hit.

The battalion holding the trenches in front of Y Wood got it altogether in the neck. I saw their trenches blown sky-high again and again when we were allowed in our own front line. I was rather proud of myself the third day. I managed a shave, and I don't know anyone else who did.

After three days in front, we spent another three days in the support trench, and I am not sure that that was not the worst of the two. It was old and dilapidated, with low parapets affording no sort of protection. It ended in a cul-de-sac, and at night I held the last traverse. In the daytime we were not allowed to use the two end traverses, as they were considered too dangerous, and we had to crowd into those farther down.

Each day two sections were ordered into a culvert under the Menin Road, which was also used as a first-aid post. I spent one day there. A stream ran through the culvert and we had to sit on our packs against the wall, without much chance of moving more than a few inches. It was a blazing hot day, and through each end of the culvert we could see the glare of the sunshine on the trees and the almost continual bursting of the shells. The Huns were using a certain number of armour-piercing shells on the road, and if one had happened to catch the road above us, we should have found ourselves like rats in a trap. All day increasing numbers of wounded were brought in, and the narrow space became more and more congested.

We were usually warned of the hours of special energy; but they always commenced a few moments too early, and over and over again we were nearly caught. The last evening things were a trifle quieter, and we had an early visit from men of the battalion who were to relieve us and who had come to inspect the position. Just before we left, one of their ration parties was paraded on the Menin Road, and was caught by a big shrapnel which laid out some score of them. When we did get away, my section was paraded at the same spot, and I wasn't sorry to move off.

12*th October*, 1915.

I have had a stroke of luck and have been taking a well-deserved holiday, although I say it myself. When we came out, we marched to the Dickebusche Field, to be held in reserve, if necessary. The next day I found myself a Lance-Sergeant. We had lost so many sergeants during the six days that promotion was rapid.

Two days later we moved on to a new transport field, an entirely new abode, filled with huts of wood, where we were much more comfortable than we should have been in the open. It was very wet and our roof leaked, but we did not remain there long.

At 10.30 p.m. on the 2nd we were suddenly ordered to pack up and stand by, ready to march at fifteen minutes' notice. We lay in the huts and tried to get some sleep, but heard no more until 4.30 in the morning, when the order came to parade in marching order at once. We had to leave half of our stuff behind, as parcels had just arrived, and either the local natives or the next unit in possession had the benefit of it.

It was the first time that I had ever marched

up in the daylight. We were only about two hundred strong, and, much to our disgust, half-way up to Ypres we passed a new Kitchener battalion, thirteen hundred strong, coming out. For some reason, best known to themselves, they jeered at us.

We marched by way of a long communication trench, which wound through Zillebeke Village and round the Lake. Near the village we halted for an hour or two, and there we heard that the Huns had exploded a mine in Sanctuary Wood and occupied the crater, and we were required as reinforcements. With us were the last few men left of the Liverpool Scottish, who had been badly cut up in the attack.

We were ordered to leave our packs in the communication trench, with a guard who would collect them. I never saw mine again. This order sounded ominous, and a short time after we started the word was sent down the line that "the Jocks would fight without bonnets to-day". It was suspected that the Huns would use the uniforms of some Jock prisoners, whom they had captured.

At last we reached the end of the communication trench and entered Sanctuary Wood. I had seen it a score of times before, but it was so changed as to be almost unrecognizable. Old lines of trenches had disappeared. Old dugouts had been

Dugouts in Maple Copse, Hooge, October, 1915

[To face page 214

swept away and new ones had taken their places. The only landmark that remained was the little cemetery between the two woods, with its white wooden crosses gleaming in the sunshine.

In the end the affair became a very mixed up one, and it was difficult to ascertain what was happening. We got into a part of the wood which I did not know, and after passing along a front-line trench, we were left in a maze of little communication or drainage trenches, only two or three feet deep and surrounded by thick underbrush, which must have been a few yards in the rear of the captured line.

One could see nothing and only the bombs told us where the front really was. Our own guns delivered half an hour's bombardment to commence with. We got the benefit of a good deal of it, and a jagged piece of falling shell cut my hand. It may have been one of our own or one of the enemy's. I twisted a handkerchief around it, but almost at once a flat piece of shell caught the knuckles of the same hand, and for the greater part of the day it was quite dead and useless.

Then a bombing attack was made, in which the principal part was taken by our own bombers. I believe they drove the Huns out of most of their gains, but it was quite impossible to tell exactly what was happening, even in the immediate neighbourhood. We sat in or on the edge of our baby trenches all day long, amidst a constant rain of debris. Every few minutes messages were received from someone to someone, and passed down somewhere. " Pass down that our shells are falling short." " Our shells very short." " All wires down, have sent on runner." " Stretcher-bearers wanted at once." " Send up more bombs." " More rifle ammunition wanted." " Must have more bombs." " Stretchers wanted, two bad cases." " Are there any Jocks in the firing-line?" " Send up more bombers." " Two platoons of the Z——s wanted to reinforce on the left." " Send up more bombs."

Bag after bag of bombs was passed up, and sling after sling of ammunition, by a dozen at a time. This seemed to go on interminably most of the day, and all the time the Hun guns were searching the wood with some of the heaviest stuff that I have experienced. At one time the bombs began to fall amongst us, but this attack was apparently beaten off. At any rate the falling bombs receded, and after darkness fell the uproar began to die down and finally ceased altogether, except for an occasional shell which fell in the wood, but came from Heaven knows where.

My Platoon Sergeant was wounded early in the day and I was left in charge, so I could not worry about my hand until late at night. About 10.0, everything being quiet, I thought I might as well go down and get it properly dressed. After some difficulty I got leave to do so, and leaving the next senior N.C.O. in charge, I started down through the wood. I lost my way once, but finally reached a dressing-station just on the edge of the wood. There I found a wounded officer with his back torn to pieces, having it dressed by an orderly. No one else was there, and after waiting for some time I was told to go on to our own dressing-station in Maple Copse.

Just outside, I found four of our own men, pretty badly wounded, but walking cases, who were bound in the same direction but did not know the way. I guided them to the Copse with some difficulty, having to climb in and out of several choked-up trenches on the way. After searching round, we discovered another dressing-station, which proved to be that of the Royal Scots. No one could tell us where our own place was, so we waited about, and after a time an M.O. had a look at us.

The others he sent off to the ambulance at once. He asked me what was the matter, and on my telling him that I had merely a shell scratch on the hand, he said that in any case I must be inoculated, and I had better walk over to Gordon Farm, the point where the ambulances waited.

About thirty men were waiting about outside, so I more or less took charge, and led them, ploughing our way through six inches of mud, up to the farm. Here we were packed into an ambulance almost at once, and rushed through Ypres to Branthoec, where there was a Field Ambulance Station. It was a bumpy ride, as the Menin Road and Ypres itself were not healthy spots in which to linger, and we went at full speed all the way.

At the Station I had a big bowl of hot cocoa and an orderly came round and pricked us all in the breast, against tetanus. Another ambulance trip brought us to No. 7 Field Hospital, at the back of Poperinghe, where we arrived about 2.0 in the morning, and after a bowl of soup my hand was dressed and I turned in in a tent for the rest of the night.

In the morning we were inspected, and although I assured everyone that I had only a scratch, I was told that I must go on to hospital at Haasbrouek, and thither we went by ambulance about midday. It was quite a comfortable spot, and as I did not feel in the least degree ill, I rather enjoyed it.

As I had lost all my belongings, I asked for leave to go into the town on Sunday afternoon in order to buy a razor and other things. I had some trouble to get it, but my sergeant's stripes stood me in very good stead, and in the end I succeeded and spent a pleasant afternoon wandering round the town. I never realized before what a pull three stripes give one. Luckily I had managed to get a set from another chap the previous Wednesday, and had had them sewn on by a girl at a farm where we had had a meal. They made all the difference. As a sergeant they would do anything for me.

The nurses were charming, all ladies, and the matron, who had had a parcel of underclothing from home, gave me socks and an extra shirt. Just fancy! It was the first time since last Christmas that I have heard the voice of an Englishwoman.

The town was a ripping little place and everyone I met was so courteous, so keen to do anything for me, so cheerful, so different from those sullen semi-German peasants of Flanders. It quite bucked me up.

It was a most extraordinary change to be able to go into a shop and be received with smiles, instead of sullen glances. At one shop I was asked into their private room and given a drink of wine, while I played with the baby of the family.

The next morning I got my discharge. An Irish private from our division was placed under my charge, and we were told to take the train for Poperinghe at 4.0 o'clock. The private went off on his own business, promising to meet me at the station, and I myself wandered round the town.

It was market day and the town was full of country folk. At lunch-time, when I went to the hotel, I had much ado to find a seat. In the end I found myself at a round table in a small room with five French farmers. They were bent on having a good time and insisted on including me in it. Each in turn ordered a bottle of wine of a different sort, and we each had a small glass from every bottle. I wound up by standing them liqueurs, and by the time we had finished I had to make for the station in a hurry. We parted the best of friends.

At the station I found my private rather the worse for his potations, but I managed to get him into the train, and he slept until we reached Poperinghe, just on dusk. There a large new draft had just arrived for some battalion, and as the Huns were shelling the railhead, things were in some confusion. We got away from the neighbourhood as quickly as possible and found our way across country to the transport field. My private's battalion was resting on the other side of the road, so I had no trouble with him after I had once got him safely out of the town.

I reported to the Quartermaster, who told me that the battalion would be coming out of the line

in a few days, and if I liked I might await their
return in the transport field, so for a few more
days I lived in comfort.

I found that as I had got to the wrong dressing-
station they had lost trace of me, and I was thought
to have come to grief on my way through the wood
and had been posted as missing. Unluckily all my
letters had been returned, marked "Hospital", and
in due time will go back to the senders.

I spent the next few days in great comfort and
dignity, messing with the C.Q.M.S. and the
Company cooks, wandering round the country-side
and eating the bread of idleness. I even discovered
some sportsmen amongst the transport, who
enjoyed a quiet game of cards, and I believe I
was actually getting fat when the battalion came
out to rest.

The Adjutant was one of the first to arrive, and
from him I heard that we had done with the giddy
old Salient and were to go to the rear for a long
rest. The next day, however, we were told that
the Salient would never desert Mr. Micawber and
that we were to go up again in the usual course.

*23rd October*, 1915.

After all, we didn't have a bad time. Everyone had the wind-up, for we all felt it was our last tour in the horrid Salient, and anything might happen. We went up to a trench in Square Wood, between Hill 60 and Maple Copse. The Huns strafed heavily on each side of us and showers of shells fell on our old quarters in Sanctuary Wood, but I don't believe that a single shell was aimed at our location. The worst thing about it was the march up and back. It was ten miles each way, and two of them through a communication trench.

In the trench itself we had no dugout, but I managed to sleep for five hours curled up under a parapet. Our predecessors seem to have had some arrangement with the Huns not to fire, for at first they were very cheeky, and their working parties came right out into the open in broad daylight. A shot or two put that right, however, and afterwards neither side troubled the other over much. We were right on the edge of a sort of precipice, up which zigzagged the approach to the trench, so the ground at the immediate rear was absolutely "dead" and as safe as could be.

The trench proved the most cushy in the Salient, and so far as I can hear, we had not a single casualty.

It took us six hours to cover the ten miles back. For one thing, we lost our way in the fields near Zillebeke Lake and could not find a way out until we heard the pipes of the Gordons playing their men down a road only a hundred yards away.

In the transport field it appeared to be an accepted fact that we were not to go in again. Our brigade was to be disbanded, the units going to other divisions. Still, for the time being, we were to be "considered available, if required, in the firing-line".

At night most of the men go up digging, and two hundred of us are up in Ypres on a salvage job. The rest of us spend the day assisting the Engineers in the fortification of farms in the good old way.

I have just had a narrow squeak of it! Only one man in the Company is going home on Saturday, and that man am I. My pass has come, and I have only half an hour in which to reach Poperinghe and catch my train.

**THE END**

Printed in Great Britain
by Amazon

58776627R00149